The Pa

A One Hundred Day Journey

by
Michelle Griffin-Carter

DORRANCE
PUBLISHING CO
EST. 1920
PITTSBURGH, PENNSYLVANIA 15238

Dorrance Publishing Co
585 Alpha Drive
Suite 103
Pittsburgh, PA 15238
Visit our website at *www.dorrancebookstore.com*

ISBN: 979-8-8860-4269-6
eISBN: 979-8-8860-4540-6

The Paradigm Shift:

A One Hundred Day Journey

by

Michelle Griffin-Carter

Introduction

Life can be viewed as a journey; along the way there will be many encounters of life-altering events. There will be trying moments that will test our moral character and moments that will shift the outcome of our future. However life-altering these events will be, we must learn how to navigate through them properly, resulting in the fulfillment of our divine purpose. While embarking on your journey, every so often there will be moments within a person's life where they will have a spiritual awakening, moments where people say that they have heard from God about the condition of their lives and even the world around them. Well, this very experience occurred. Toward the end of one decade and entering the beginning of a new decade, I had a spiritual encounter with God. During this encounter God spoke to me about a paradigm shift about to occur, a shift within the atmosphere where there will be a series of unexplained events. The world as we knew it would no longer be the same. Unsure as to what was happening to me, I decided to write everything down in a journal as I walked and talked with God on a one-hundred-day journey.

Before embarking on any journey, we must first seek wise counsel. "Hear counsel, and receive instruction, that thou mayest be wise in thy latter end" (Proverbs 19:20 NIV). Prior to writing this journal I sought a higher authority or wise counsel and shared what God had spoken to me. My instructions were to ensure that I journal well. It was imperative for me to continue to pray and study the Word of God and make certain I was indeed hearing from God.

Day One

January 14, 2020

Today marks the first day of the one-hundred-day journey. There is a paradigm shift, a major shift within the atmosphere that is about to occur. Before I continue, I will have to go back a few years, maybe even a decade to explain exactly what a paradigm shift is, what can occur, and how to prepare. It was almost a year ago that God spoke to me about a paradigm shift. However, it was on January 13, 2020, when God said to me, one hundred days. The next one hundred days are crucial and will prove to be life changing. It is imperative that during this time everyone is in alignment and in the right place because when the shift occurs you do not want to miss it.

I am reminded of a Bible story, a parable of the ten virgins (Matthew 25:1–13). There were ten virgins in this story. Five virgins were foolish and unprepared for the arrival of the bridegroom and did not bring extra oil with them, only their pre-lit lamps. However, the five wise virgins carried their pre-lit lamps and extra oil to be prepared because they did not know the exact day or hour the bridegroom would arrive.

While waiting the virgins fell asleep and the bridegroom arrived at midnight. The foolish virgins who were unprepared ran out of oil and were unable to meet him because they had to go buy more oil. However, the wise virgins that carried extra oil with them were able to meet the bridegroom because they were prepared. When the other five virgins finally arrived, the door was shut, and they were sent away because they missed their opportunity. During these next one hundred days it is imperative not to miss your opportunity during the paradigm shift. You have to be in position, continue to remain focused, stay in the word, "Draw nigh to God and he will draw nigh to you" (James 4:8 KJV).

Prior to this moment God was dealing with me on a few things. I was out of alignment and about to lose everything of any significant value, which was my family. Therefore, it was imperative for me to submit fully to God and remain obedient. "Submit yourselves, then, to God. Resist the devil, and he will flee from you. Come near to God and he will come near to you. Wash your hands, you sinners, and purify your hearts, you double-minded. Grieve, mourn and wail. Change your laughter to mourning and your joy to gloom. Humble yourselves before the Lord, and he will lift you up" (James 4:7–10 NIV). I understand that the road ahead is going to be long, and I must be a willing participant and complete the transformation process.

Day Two

January 15, 2020

In order to achieve spiritual growth a paradigm shift is required. A paradigm shift is a change from one way of thinking to another and can apply to anything on earth or in your daily life. According to biblical history there were twelve major paradigm shifts in the Bible. One major shift was a change in who was considered to be God's people. In the Old Testament God's people were originally the children of Israel or the Jews. The lineage of God's people descended from a common ancestor, Jacob, who was the son of Isaac, who was the son of Abraham.

Although anyone could worship God it was a special gift to have a direct lineage, giving you an advantage over anyone else. However, in the New Testament there was a paradigm shift and God's people came from many nations, not born of blood or the will of flesh, or man, but of God. "He came to his own, and his own received him not, but as many as received him, to them gave he power to become the sons of God, even to them that believe on his name: Which were born, not of blood, nor of the will of the flesh, nor of the will of man, but of God" (John 1:11-14 KJV).

The paradigm shift can be viewed as a transformative process. During the paradigm shift one can literally experience or go through a transformation process. My transformation process began at the end of 2019. However, I was thrust into this process due to a series of traumatic events that occurred decades ago.

Day Three

January 16, 2020

I went for my daily walk today, and while walking I received a phone call from a friend. We began to talk, and the conversation quickly turned. I continued to listen as they shared with me what God said, as they completely dismissed the reality of their situation. I understand that at the end of the day people really don't want to hear the truth. People say, tell me the truth even if it hurts me, which is an honest lie. For if I tell you the truth, I might not only hurt you, but I could cause your entire world to come crashing down with the truth. The issue is everyone does not live in reality. People are stuck in a fantasy world that they have created and call it faith and who am I to bust the bubble of people.

Who am I to shatter the dreams of those who see reality but refuse to accept it? After all, isn't that what faith is, the substance of things hoped for and the evidence of things not seen. I recall one day I was praying to God to be married to this man. I wanted so badly to be with him, and God said to me, "Why are you praying for someone I am trying to protect you from?" "Will you again put a man before me?" God said, "No. What you desire you cannot have, and if you touch him again you will forfeit your future. So you can grow old waiting or do the work that I called you to do." I was having faith believing in God for something that never belonged to me. In my mind I saw what I wanted to see. I took what I saw and heard and ran with it. Not realizing that putting anything before God is wrong, putting all my time and energy into someone or something before God and not giving that same amount of energy toward my relationship with God, will forfeit anything God promised. God is a jealous God, and you cannot put anything before Him; your spouse, your job, family, nothing can come before God. Whatever gets more time or attention in your life before God, God will remove it out of your life.

My friend that called me today will always be understood by me because I have experienced something they are presently facing, and when you are in something you cannot see what those outside of the situation see, and in life we all have to reach certain levels of understanding on our own. This phone call today was enlightening. I am facing a different challenge. However, it took another person on the outside to observe what I missed because I was wrapped up in the situation. Thankfully I wasn't too deep into it that I could not receive the truth. In order for us to receive the truth we have to be healthy enough in our thinking that we cannot take things personally. Rather, we must examine ourselves and see if what is being said can be applied to any area of our life.

Day Four

January 17, 2020

During these one hundred days there will be a shifting in thought, speech, and lifestyle changes. Major changes will occur, forcing people to want to be better. Unexplained events will take place, people will have many unanswered questions and will run to the church for answers. However, what will they be running to, if the church is unrecognizable? How can we save the world if we have become like the world? There has to be a balance, therefore realignment must occur.

As a Christian, a baptized believer of Jesus Christ, I grew up in church. I was raised in the Baptist church. I was in church so much, I was even born on a Sunday. I attended Sunday school, bible study, vacation bible school, choir rehearsal, mid-week worship and church all day Sunday. I had a lot of understanding on how to have church. However, I had a limited understanding of the Word of God (the Bible). As a child attending Sunday school, I was given a good foundation. I was able to recite scripture. I could, by rote memory, tell you the number of books in the Bible and what we in the Baptist church believed.

7

We received sound doctrine, however, there wasn't a clear blueprint on how to live a Godly balanced life. I was unprepared for the world outside of church; just saying the blood of Jesus while something was coming at you was not working. I began to question my faith. Was I not spiritual enough? Did I not have the Holy Ghost power that was preached on Sunday to defeat Satan? Growing up everything was a sin. I was continuously rebuked and sent to hell with gasoline drawers on. I believed everything I was taught at home and in church as a child to be true until I began to study and read the Bible for myself. As I began to study the Bible for myself and sought wise counsel, I realized that a majority of what I was taught was "Fear Gospel."

It is imperative to understand that growing up during the 80's and 90's was a different time. Things were shifting faster than usual. New religious movements or organizations were being born. The framework of the church was changing and continued to change. A new generation was springing forth, and their viewpoint about the church and the world was no longer the same. The influence and power the church had in the community and in the world was beginning to decline. To keep the reign of power or control, our parents and elders would tell you things to scare you, in hopes that you would listen. I recall being ten years old and my mother telling me that if I ever kissed a boy I would get pregnant. I was shocked and fearful.

However, one Sunday after morning worship, before the start of the second service I went behind the old oak tree and kissed the little boy who was my fifteen-minute boyfriend. I say fifteen minutes because back then I was not allowed to have a boyfriend. We only saw each other at church, and there was only fifteen minutes in between services for us to actually be alone together. If you were gone too long the mothers of the church would send a search party out for you. After kissing this boy in front of our two best friends we ran back inside the sanctuary with the other kids to listen to the musicians get ready for the next service.

I sat there for a few seconds unable to move and then fell crashing down to the floor. I was overcome with grief and sorrow. My life was about to change, my viewpoint was about to change. Much like these next one hundred days, I was experiencing a transformation in the matter of seconds. As I fell to the floor I began to cry and holler. Everyone stopped what they were doing to see what my issue was. My cousin walked over to me and asked me what was wrong. I yelled out, "I kissed my boyfriend and now I'm pregnant." My cousin said, "Okay, you kissed him, but did you have sex?" I looked up at my cousin with tears in my eyes and a confused look on my face. I replied, "What's that?" Everyone laughed. My cousin said, "Get up, stupid. Whoever told you that lied to you." At that moment I was relieved and angry at the fact I was lied to about becoming pregnant. By not knowing the truth I was misinformed.

Day Five

January 18, 2020

It is one thing to have information and no direction. However, it is extremely dangerous to have little to no information, no direction, and you are left to your own devices, trying to feel your way through. Growing up my routine was the same: school, home, and church. Every week it was the same thing. I enjoyed my existence within my bubble. My world was good. I was happy and safe, until one day my brother came by the house and said, "All you do is go to school, church, and come back home again." I looked at him like, "Yeah, what's wrong with that?" He said there was more to life than just going to school and church all the time. I was eighteen when my brother introduced me to a world that I had never seen before. However, I was nineteen when I actually attempted to step out into that world, and the only advice I was given was to enjoy myself, take my time but enjoy.

Day Six

January 19, 2020

Up until this point of my life I had only been exposed to and taught to fear God, don't wear makeup or short skirts, don't kiss boys or you will get pregnant and go to hell with gasoline drawers on. All of these things were false. My viewpoint about life and what I believed had shifted. My experience in a world outside of church was a culture shock. I had a door cracked open that I quickly kicked down. I went from having little information to an extreme amount of information, with no direction and not wise enough to seek God for wisdom.

I was of legal age to make my own decisions; nobody was going to babysit me. If something went wrong, the response was always the same. "You should have known better. Didn't your parents teach you this already?" My response was always the same: "No." I do recall my father telling me when I was a child, "Everything in moderation." Of course, he was referring to the amount of food on my plate. If he thought I was eating too much he would always say "Everything in moderation, you don't want to be 200 plus pounds." My father's words did not serve me well because I over-indulged and gained an extreme amount of weight. However, I have finally become serious about my eating habits and living my best healthy life.

I cannot entirely say that I completely abandoned everything I was taught or my religious beliefs, because it was that teaching about sin, hell, and eternal torment that caused me to repent every time I stepped across the line. My prayer would be, "God forgive me, don't let me die. Don't send me to hell. God, please have mercy on me, give me grace like you gave your servant David in the Bible." God had mercy on me. However, I always had a reminder of what could have happened. I recall attending a function. There was a comedian performing. Our eyes connected and we were locked into each other while he performed on stage. After finishing his set he walked past every fine half-naked woman there and straight to me. The first thing this man said to me was, "You don't belong here, you're a church girl, a good girl." He said, "You are the only one here at a pajama party wearing actual pajamas and Tweety Bird slippers." We both laughed. He said, "But you got your own style, you're a breath of fresh air." We talked for a while that night. As we continued to talk, I grew tired of him telling me how good I was. So I said to him, "I'll show you how good I am."

Day Seven

January 20, 2020

God requires so much more from us. In order for us to receive our promise, we first have to do what is required of us. However, we must first know and understand what that requirement is. "But he that knew not, and did commit things worthy of stripes, shall be beaten with few stripes. For unto whomsoever much is given, of him shall be much required: and to whom men have committed much, of him they will ask the more" (Luke 12:48 KJV). I wasted a lot of time and caused a lot of my issues trying to prove to people that I wasn't so holy, that I was just like them. When the truth was, I was different. I was chosen: "You did not choose me, but I chose you and appointed you so that you might go and bear fruit—fruit that will last—and so that whatever you ask in my name the Father will give you" (John 15:16 NIV).

I could not do everything everyone else was doing, and when I tried, the consequence or penalty was great. I knew at an early age that I had to hold myself at a higher standard; I was not normal. However, I would diminish my self-worth, my value for acceptance and validation, when I should have been looking for approval from

God. I do not regret my life experiences because they allowed me to appreciate how I was raised, they helped me to grow. "For it is a poor man who does not learn from his mistakes" (Dr. Todd M. Hall, Sr.). My mistakes gave me real testimony.

True, a lot of what I went through and am currently experiencing, I caused myself. I recall my mother telling me, "God takes care of babies and fools." Well, I was a big fool and falling quickly into the place of no return. It was imperative for me to use wisdom in making decisions and obtain wisdom at any cost. "Get wisdom, get understanding; do not forget my words or turn away from them. Do not forsake wisdom, and she will protect you; love her, and she will watch over you. The beginning of wisdom is this: Get wisdom. Though it costs all you have, get understanding" (Proverbs 4: 5–7 NIV).

Unfortunately, I found myself, or should I say I entangled myself, into compromising situations. I knew I could not look to my siblings for help or assistance. They would say, "Figure it out. You got yourself into it, now get yourself out." I knew I could not go to my parents, because my father would cuss me out, and my mother would be crying, "The Blood of Jesus, why my child?" When the issue was, why didn't you teach your child about the world, tell your children the truth about sex, relationships, drugs, alcohol, managing money, life skills? I knew how to fake like I was speaking in tongues. However, I did not know how to function outside of church. Now, one might say, even if you were not taught these things, there is no excuse, you could have asked God to give you wisdom.

Day Eight

January 21, 2020

I recall having a conversation with a friend and they shared there were moments in their life when they had to learn things on their own and not expect anyone to teach them because that person was not always physically available to do so. We have to ask God for wisdom, just as Solomon asked God for wisdom to lead God's people; God gave him wisdom, wealth, possessions, and honor, such as no king before him ever had and none after him would ever have what God had given to Solomon (2 Chronicles 1:7–11). Unfortunately, sometimes people can be so used to being in a certain situation or state of mind that they do not want to change. This is an ignorant thought process but truth. I thought about what was said and the advice given. I also thought it is always easy to give advice, however, whether or not people take that advice or use it for themselves is something different altogether. I accepted what was said and remained quiet: "Not every comment warrants a response" (Dr. Todd M. Hall, Sr). My prayer is that God opens our eyes that we may see. Open our ears that we may hear from God clearly and open our hearts that we may receive His word.

Day Nine

January 22, 2020

Within these next one hundred days, we have to be careful with what flows from our mouth. I find myself having to choose my words carefully because the slip of the lip can cause a ripple of repercussions. There are many things happening around me that I don't have all the information. I have bits and pieces. Therefore, it is imperative for me to remain still and silent.

Day Ten

Even if I have all the information it is not my place to divulge that information. Sometimes you can be so full that what's on the inside spills over. I recall an old saying, "Loose lips sink ships." No need to have diarrhea of the mouth. It will only cause more problems putting you in a worse situation than you were in before. When I was supposed to exit quickly, I stayed too long, and now I have a stench of someone else's mess on my fingers. I even added my own mess. I got out only to jump right back into the mess—absolutely foolish. "As a dog returns back to its vomit, so do fools repeat their folly" (Proverbs 26:11 NIV). I am watching all of these things unravel right in front of me. God had already told me to get out while I still had time. It is true what they say: "Curiosity killed the cat," or it will at least leave you paralyzed.

I attached myself to people who had worse issues than I did. I was intrigued; I always have to see how the story ends, even when I already know the ending. Someone is always left heartbroken holding a bag of mess. While everyone else goes on living their "happily ever after." However, if I am not careful I could end up being the one holding a bag of everyone else's crap. Therefore, it is imperative to remain focused. There is so much work that needs to be done, there is no time to get caught up in the messy lives of other people or their fantasy worlds because at the end of the day they are still making their money, living their best life and life has passed you by. Some people may be nice, however, they are also unwelcomed distractions.

Day Eleven

January 24, 2020

I have to thank God for the spirit of discernment. Warning comes before destruction. "Pride goes before destruction, a haughty spirit before a fall" (Proverbs 16:18 NIV). Sometimes people are sent into your life for a specific time, reason, or season. Sometimes we have encounters with people to give or receive a message and move on. However, when we feel a connection or have something in common, we stay too long creating or developing relationships that should have never formed, causing you to get off course. During these one hundred days, time is a precious commodity. Time cannot be wasted. I must remain focused and committed to who I am accountable for. Having pointless conversations about the same thing day in and day out are mentally draining. I am starting to understand why people disappear without explanation. People can be draining. During this time it is imperative to connect with people who add value to my life. "As iron sharpens iron, so one person sharpens another" (Proverbs 27:17 NIV).

In time God will reveal all things. God does not make mistakes. During this time it feels like I have been left to die, that I have been isolated on purpose. I tried to rationalize why people walked away. However, I understand that it was necessary. I must obey God. I have been delayed because I did not obey God. God has not forgotten about me or my family. In this paradigm shift God is about to do something huge. I must walk away from my past for good and cut off anything that reminds me of my past. I remember when I was a child, and I would listen to the elders of the church say during the altar call, "Come to Jesus, take your burdens to the Lord and leave them there. Lay everything that has you bound on the altar and when you leave it there don't pick it back up."

The shift is happening right before my eyes. I knew that people were watching, I just never knew how many. Who I considered to be friends were actually foes. The more I talk to God and study His word, the more I see. It has been my prayer for God to open up my eyes that I may see, open my ears that I may hear from God clearly, and then God open up my heart, that I may receive your Word. Relationships with those I considered to be friends will end. Some relationships are beneficial, while others are detrimental. During this season of the paradigm shift, we have to be mindful of what or who we expose ourselves to. Everything good is not always good for you.

Day Twelve

January 25, 2020

My eyes have been opened. The question is what took me so long. I had stated earlier that God had spoken to me. However, it was on August 5, 2019 that I had a dream. In this dream I saw a hand coming out of the sky. It was the hand of God holding a long broom covering the whole earth. I watched the hand sweeping across the earth, and as the broom moved bodies began dropping everywhere and were swept away under the broom. As the bodies began to be swept away a new crop of people were springing up from the ground, a small remnant that replaced the ones who were swept away.

I woke up and I immediately told my husband about the dream, and I said God was going to do a clean sweep. I said that people were going to die and be exposed by God and then wiped out. I said we have to repent and ask God for mercy. I said that it is starting to happen now, but you will really begin to see it in January 2020 throughout the entire year into January 2021. Those who have been wiped out will be replaced by God's remnant and that no one is exempt. We must repent. God's grace and mercy cannot be played with. People are deceiving themselves by thinking because God didn't take them out while they were sinning that it is okay to sin. No, it is not okay. We must repent and change. We cannot afford to be double minded: "A double minded man is unstable in all his ways" (James 1:8 KJV). People are going to be running back to God because of the unexplained things, but the church needs to be detoxed. How can the people be saved if the church is not saved or delivered itself? The infection has to be exposed in order to receive the cure; the cure has to be pure and it is rare. Warning comes before destruction. "Pride goes before destruction, a haughty spirit before a fall" (Proverbs 16:18 NIV). I have been chosen to tell the story as I view it. Be still, be silent, and write.

Day Thirteen

January 26, 2020

"All day long I've been with Jesus all day long I have been with him." That song has been in my spirit. I was sitting in the afternoon service today, when a text message came across my phone. It was a group text with my family. My nephew texted that Kobe Bryant was killed in a plane crash. Then he texted again stating that Kobe's thirteen-year-old daughter was with him and lost her life as well. We later found out that the aircraft they were in was a helicopter, and everyone on board died a total of nine people. My first thought was, "Did he know Jesus? Was he saved?" I replied to the text with, "We must pray for his family and continue to pray for everyone." People are confused about all these unexplained deaths. He was so young, his daughter, the other people on the aircraft. People are not going to understand what is going on and they will be seeking answers and we have to be in position, we have to be ready because what is about to happen is bigger than us.

Day Fourteen

January 27, 2020

People are so pressed to be married, obtain success, and achieve their goals. However, after we die all of those things will not matter anymore. We can obtain so much wealth, build houses only to die, and never get a chance to fully enjoy the fruits of our labor. "For a person may labor with wisdom, knowledge and skill, and then must leave all they own to another who has not toiled for it. This too is meaningless and a great misfortune" (Ecclesiastes 2:21 NIV). Then you have some people who live a long life and have not accomplished anything. We all have a set time, a time to be born, a time to mourn, a time to love, a time to live, and a time to die, however, it's what we chose to do with that time that matters the most (Ecclesiastes 3). Time is the only thing in this world that you cannot get back. Once it's gone, it is gone.

Every day that we wake up our time is extended. No one knows when our time is done. I can no longer afford to waste time. Almost thirty-eight years on this earth and I have wasted so much time. I allowed my unhealthy thought process and poor habits to diminish my time. I must remain focused and continue my journey toward destiny. I had fallen asleep this morning after the kids left for school. I had a dream. In this dream I was still staying at my current hotel, and I was there with my husband, when I received an Uber alert to pick up a woman that was going on a long trip. She was going to Philadelphia and then New York. I accepted the trip, and the fare was six hundred dollars. The woman called me and asked how long it would take me to get to her pick-up location. I told her that the GPS states that I will arrive at her location within thirty minutes.

She told me to take my time and stated that she would give me a two-hundred-dollar tip if I took her further than the first two destinations, and the entire trip would add up to twelve hundred and seventy-five dollars. I told my husband about the trip, and he said that he was coming with me. I said I wasn't sure if he could come with me. He said yes, "You can drive your car, I will follow you, park my car, and then ride with you." I agreed and we left. I arrived at the first location to pick the woman up. I asked her if it was okay for my husband to come.

She said "No," that we were headed to destiny. She said, "You have to take me to destiny. No one else can come." She said that I have to take this journey alone. I woke up from the dream, and I was confused because currently I do not have a car, and my husband is the one who works with Uber. Aside from the numbers or amounts for the specific destinations, what stood out for me the most was the statement, "I must take this journey alone, no one else can come. You have to take me to destiny." I do not have a full interpretation of this dream at this time. However, God will reveal all things in time. I understand that everyone cannot come with you on your journey, and there will be moments along the way where you are just passing through to give or receive an encouraging word to or from someone and continue on your journey.

Day Fifteen

January 28, 2020

Along with testimonies of death and destruction, there will be great testimonies of victories and miracles. For we cannot have one without the other. I'm reminded of an old song by Frankie Beverly & Maze: "Joy and Pain, Sunshine and Rain." These things have to occur. It is not about what we obtain on this earth but rather how we impact the lives of other people. What will be your legacy when you leave the earth? Would you have fulfilled your divine purpose, who will celebrate you, chant your name in the street? Who will remember you long after you are gone? Therefore, it is imperative to make the best of your time on earth. Time cannot be wasted.

Day Sixteen

January 29, 2020

The struggle is definitely real. When embarking on your journey, be prepared to be tested. "A faith not tested can't be trusted" (Dr. Todd M. Hall, Sr.). Today I failed my test, my thoughts were plagued by the past. I didn't reach back, however, I did not control my thoughts—I battled within my mind going into flash-back mode. We have to stand firm in our position, choose a stance, and stick with it. We cannot waiver in our faith. Above anything else our prayer life has to be strong. We have to be mentally and spiritually strong enough to block out unwelcome distractions. There will be weak moments, but we must continue to fight. So much time wasted, so much work left undone. You don't want to be caught with your work undone.

Day Seventeen

January 30, 2020

I was listening to the news, and it was reported that the United States has its first case of someone testing positive for person-to-person transmission of coronavirus—a man who returned to the United States after visiting China. No one is really sure how this virus was created and why it's spreading so quickly. The World Health Organization is declaring the coronavirus outbreak to be a public health emergency of international concern. Of course, the White House is saying we shouldn't worry, everything is under control. Only God really knows.

There are things happening around us that we will not fully understand. However, in time God will reveal all things. I had another dream today. I didn't quite understand the meaning. I gave the message to the person, and I'm sure they understood the meaning. However, I slipped up again. I was just supposed to give the message and move on. Instead I continued to want to strike up a conversation replaying old events back in my mind. Soul ties are crazy, some people say you just have to walk away completely. I didn't pass this test. Just because God showed me something does not necessarily mean I have to say anything. "Because He shows it does not mean you have to share it. Some things are shown for us to intercede to make sure that what we see, especially if it's negative never occurs" (Dr. Todd M. Hall, Sr.). I get these urges and want to say what I am seeing. Maybe God was testing me to see if I could control my urge to reach out when no one else is reaching back, unless it is beneficial to them.

Day Eighteen

January 31, 2020

After I had the dream about transporting a woman to different locations, I decided to look closely at the meaning of the distance, time, and fare amounts. I prayed, asking God to give me understanding of the meaning of the dream. I began by researching the numbers in the dream and their specific meaning. I looked up the meaning of the number 1,275, which was the total amount I would receive after completing my journey. The number 1,275 represents life-altering changes that will affect all aspects of my life. It is imperative to remain enthusiastic and motivated as I continue on the journey of fulfilling my divine purpose.

The significance and meaning of the number 1,275 is to recognize the life changes that are currently happening, allow them to occur because they are the right ones and have the capacity to transform my life completely. In Greek the number 1,275 means over and over again (intermittently) or always (without interruption). The first number or the amount in the dream was 600. The number 600 symbolizes spiritual development, balance of home and family. The number 600 represents the changes of life cycles and phases. The number 200, which was the tip, represents hard work, or everything I have worked hard for is going to become a reality, and I will be prepared for whatever is coming my way. The number 475 was the additional fare for going the extra distance to destiny. The number 475 in Hebrew means, "God restores." Four hundred and seventy-five also means, "The Lord gives life."

The number thirty was the amount of time that it would take me to pick up the passenger from my current location. Biblically the number thirty symbolizes a man's dedication to work or to do a certain task. Jesus began to publicly preach at the age of thirty, "Now Jesus himself was about thirty years old when he began his ministry," (Luke 3:23 NIV). It is believed that thirty is the age when a person is ready and mature enough to take on responsibility: "Count all the men from thirty to fifty years of age who come to serve in the work at the tent of meeting," (Numbers 4:3 NIV). In other words, "you are now ready," you can be trusted with taking on difficult tasks, and handle what is about to occur in your life. In my quest to understand the meaning and the significance of the numbers, I looked up the meaning of the word "destiny" and the distance between each location of the trip.

According to the Merriam-Webster dictionary, "destiny" can be defined as the events that will occur to a particular person or thing in the future, certain fortune, fate. "Destiny" is what's meant to be, inescapable fate. "Destiny" is synonymous with other nouns like divine decree, fortune, and serendipity. There is no avoiding destiny, it is going to happen no matter what you do. However good or bad, destiny will occur. However, when you are face-to-face with destiny, it's not about what occurred, rather, it is about how we react to what has occurred. "Life is ten percent of what happens to you and ninety percent of how you respond" (Lou Holtz).

To dream of driving a vehicle, for me, represented having full control of decision-making or the direction of a situation. Our destiny is controlled by our decisions. In the dream I was in the driver's seat of my own car navigating and controlling my direction toward destiny. It was imperative for me to follow the navigation system and ensure that every turn was made with precision. My first location in the dream was from Maryland to Philadelphia. The distance from Maryland to Philadelphia is 119 miles. Biblically the number 119 means, "the perfect sacrifice." "Blessed are those whose ways are blameless, who walk according to the law of the LORD" (Psalm 119:1 NIV), sin covering and deliverance. "Blessed is he whose transgression is forgiven, whose sin is covered" (Psalm 32:1 KJV). My sins are forgiven, and I am covered. Glory to the Lamb of God. The distance from Philadelphia to New York is ninety-four miles. The number ninety-four symbolizes good organization, sticking to the plan or following the steps that lead to your goals. When adding the two numbers together, 119 and 94, the sum was 213. In Hebrew the number 213 means to press, be pressed, make haste. Whatever God is doing and going to do in my life, He is about to put some speed on it. Hallelujah.

Day Nineteen

February 1, 2020

The message: So after doing the research and writing everything down and putting all of the pieces together, the message was clear. God was reminding me that he has not forgotten about me, that He is about to reward me for my faithfulness. God is bringing me into destiny. I have helped others and sown into the lives of many. I labored on the altar and cried out to God for His remnant. I am about to reap the fruits of my harvest. I shall have increase and overflow. What God is about to do is going to be huge. I will continuously sit and eat from the King's table. My blessing, my inheritance from God will be never ending, and it will allow me to fulfill my divine purpose on this earth. Everything is now coming into alignment for me. Everything I prayed for, everything I have put my hand to is about to be manifested. Whatever I ask for in this season, in this decade, I can have and will have effortlessly.

Therefore, I must complete the journey, follow God's navigation system for my life, and complete the transformation process because it is necessary. Transformation has to occur in order for us to fulfill our divine purpose in life, and if we complete the process, complete the transformation, we shall be rewarded. Our reward may not necessarily be monetary or worldly things. However, our reward is greater than earthly treasures. Once we willingly complete the transformation process, we will have a new mindset and be well equipped to fulfill our divine purpose focusing on destiny, and in doing so those other things of this world will be extra added unto us. "But seek ye first the kingdom of God, and his righteousness; and all these things shall be added unto you" (Matthew 6:33 KJV).

Day Twenty

February 2, 2020

Throughout this process, I have been able to observe the behavior of others and those closest to me. People, by nature, are very interesting creatures. They are creatures of habit. However, with the paradigm shift those old habits are starting to die hard. Things or circumstances are forcing people to change. This whole process is for us to fulfill our divine purpose. We must understand what our divine life purpose is and take the necessary steps to fulfill that purpose.

Day Twenty-One

February 3, 2020

One of the most difficult things to do is completely put your trust in God, and that is only difficult because of fear of not knowing. When you cannot see something, you question what is happening, and doubt and disbelief will begin to creep in. However, when you finally let go and commit to completely trusting God it can be a beautiful experience. Completely trusting God doesn't have to be hard, but we make it hard. I recall staying in Gaithersburg last year, and I was talking to God, and He said, "Be still and be silent." Not fully understanding at the time that meant God was controlling my situation. I physically didn't have to do anything but sit silently, watch, pray, and allow God to fix my situation. However, when we put our hands on it or touch something prematurely, we mess up and can potentially disqualify our future.

I have never been much of a patient person and became accustomed to getting my way or controlling things or people around me. The words "no" or "wait" were like curse words to me. Whenever I was faced with a problem or challenge, I would find a way to figure it out because there was always a sense of urgency.

I knew I had faith in God, I knew that my steps were ordered by God. I would talk to God, read the Bible, go to worship service, however, it wasn't until 2016 when I had an encounter, a spiritual awakening that would shift my thought process about my life and the direction I was heading.

Day Twenty-Two

February 4, 2020

People say leave the past behind you and move forward into the future. The old folks used to say don't burn all of your bridges. When I was a child we used to sing this song in preschool, "Make new friends but keep the old, one is silver and the other is gold." I say you have to decipher which relationships are really worth keeping and which ones to let go. After getting married I stopped talking to a lot of people. However, I did not fully cut them out of my life. Some relationships can start out as something purely physical and can turn into a genuine friendship. However, those types of relationships are rare because ninety-five percent of the time, if a relationship starts out with just sex that is really all the relationship is going to be. Then you have relationships where you start out as friends and become sexually intimate, and when the romance is gone, you breakup and one person can't move past the breakup, it is difficult to remain friends. Therefore, ruining your friendship because your head and heart were unable to separate the two.

I am not perfect. I have a few skeletons in my closet, and if any person tells you they never did anything wrong, they don't have skeletons in their closet, that is a pure lie straight from the pits of hell. My bishop used to say, "If you don't have skeletons in your closet then you got a whole body and it's stinking" (Bishop Curtis G. Norton, Sr.). A whole body just in there decaying. I have kept in contact with a few people in my life, male in particular, which my husband felt I should not have even bothered to communicate with. I kept in contact with them not because I wanted to continue to have a sexual relationship with them. However, I kept in contact with them because I knew they could connect me to people I wouldn't normally have access to. Now I will be transparent and say that there were one or two individuals that should have never had access to me because they only had one agenda. In being transparent, I gave into that agenda, not because I was starved for attention. However, they had something that I wanted, and in being immature I gave into my selfish thinking with no thought as to what my decision would really cost me, or how many lives would be affected by my decision making.

Once I commit to something fully, I am all in, there is no turning back for me. If I decide to do something I am going to do it. I have always been bold, jumping in the water before seeing how deep it was, sink or swim. I have had some near-death experiences where I almost drowned and didn't have to. We make things so much more complicated than it has to be. Today I spoke with two friends briefly, one just so happened to be my first love and the other my last. My old friend, my first love, was his usual self. I texted just to say happy birthday, he replied with a thank you and emoji heart face, which was sweet. However, when he asked me if we could talk, I knew exactly what he wanted. Now one might say why even bother, I am no longer attracted to him sexually. I know who he is. When a man shows you his true colors take notice and proceed with caution.

Anyway, we spoke over the phone, I immediately told him I knew what he wanted, and I was not going there with him. I then asked him what was going on because the only time he reaches out is when he and his wife are having issues. That seems to be a pattern with my married male friends who call me for advice as if I am a guru. I'm not because I am still trying to figure out this marriage thing or the institution of marriage myself. The issue is, some people who are married, including myself, are still thinking and living like we are single and there are single people who are thinking and living like they are married wanting to be in a covenant. I continued to talk with my friend, and we flirted a little bit. I even sent a picture to remind him of what he walked away from, boosting my ego. If you think women don't like their ego boosted, that's a lie.

We continued to talk, and he told me that after five years he and his wife were getting divorced. Before I could ask why, he quickly began to tell me that they were both in agreement that they were just not happy. When he explained to me the reasoning behind their decision, I shook my head because after thirteen years of marriage, my husband and I both have legitimate reasons to divorce each other. However, we are presently still together, still married. We have gone to counseling and making every effort to be better. However, whether we remain married or not will depend upon both of us being willing to fight for our marriage. Is what we have worth fighting for, or are we married just for the well-fare of our children or staying married just to say we are married? When the real issue is, that we are not just married but in a covenant. When my friend told me that they constantly fight over money, that there is no "we," it is always "I" or "me" when it comes to his wife. I asked if anyone cheated because people are people and I understand that things happen. I recall several years ago making a statement to my husband about another couple. I said, "Why get married and cheat?" It was not until my marriage was exposed to outside interference, that I had to eat my words. My thought process about marriage and commitment shifted, and I knew that I would never be the same again.

Day Twenty-Three

February 5, 2020

After talking to my friend, I thought about what was said and came to the conclusion that even at his age he has not yet developed a complete understanding of the covenant of marriage. His viewpoint from when we first met nineteen years ago had not changed. It has been nineteen years, and he is still thinking about his own happiness. Now I cannot say that he has not changed at all. There have been a few changes that have occurred: he has given his life to Christ, started going to Bible study and even joined a church. All of this transpired after I finally walked away for good. I no longer wanted to play his cat-and-mouse game of manipulation. Again, I say, if a man shows you his true colors take notice and proceed with caution. I am not saying that people can't change, because they can. It took me walking away from him for him to change and he actually called me to inform me that he had. I was happy for him and proud of the progress he was making.

However, I had already moved on. My thought process had shifted, I was no longer holding on to empty promises of us getting married and having a son together. He couldn't guarantee commitment, and he certainly couldn't guarantee what the sex of our child would be. During that season of my life, I realized my worth and knew that I wanted and deserved better. The issue was, at that time he was not ready to be a husband because a transformation process had to occur, and he had to be a willing participant of that process. Even after his process of transformation was complete, I understand that he was and is not supposed to be my husband. He is not a part of my process, my journey leading me to destiny. I thought about how many opportunities I missed because I was holding on to something that I should have let go years earlier. For things to change, a shift has to occur. When the paradigm shift occurs, for it to fully manifest in our lives, we must first be willing participants and embrace the transformation process.

Day Twenty- Four

February 6, 2020

Today was a day that didn't quite go as planned. I was extra tired today. I received a phone call from a friend today. We chatted for a minute, and I listened and shared a few things and they offered some good advice. I was supposed to have a meeting, however, the other party needed to reschedule. I started my dinner early, spoke with my husband, and after I finished cooking, I went to the gym. My conversation with my husband was sweet. However, when I returned from the gym the atmosphere in the house was off. I had seen my husband and the kids by the elevator outside the gym. My husband was having a verbal exchange with our eldest child. I watched as they argued with each other. I stepped off the treadmill and walked outside of the gym to listen closely to what they were saying. I asked what was going on, what occurred to cause them to be upset, but they did not respond. They were both emotionally wrapped up into their heated exchange.

As the wife and mother of this family, I set the tone of my house. I walked back inside the gym, and after finishing my workout I went back upstairs to gauge the temperature of the house. I walked in, and my husband was sitting at the table eating the food I had prepared. I asked if the food was pleasing to him, and he said it was great. The kids thought it was a little spicy. I tried to off-set the spice with a little sugar. I tasted the food before I finished cooking. However, I was more concerned about my husband's response than the kids. My husband is very picky, and if he doesn't like something he is quick to make a comment and point out any of your mistakes or how he would have done something. These last few years have been draining. I have felt like nothing I'm doing is ever enough. I stopped doing certain things because I grew tired of him complaining and never being completely satisfied or being compared to someone else. When I could just as easily tell him that I'm not completely satisfied in certain areas and compare him to someone else. That would not only bruise his ego but cause further damage to an already fragile relationship. We have torn each other down and controlled each other with manipulation and mental games. I read the kids a Bible story this evening as their bedtime story. I read the book of Esther 1-2, and as I was reading, I became convicted. I was reading and got to the part of the story in Esther 1:12–22, when Queen Vashti refused to appear before the king and disrespected him.

The part that convicted me was her disrespect and King Xerxes' reaction and his decree against her. The king's men stated that something had to be done about Vashti because other women in the province would think it is okay to publicly disrespect their husbands. At that moment I paused because I have been a poor example as a wife and mother to my husband and children, and now they think it is okay for them to do the same and when I correct them they say, "But you don't do it, you talk to Dad the same way all the time." In my defense I would tell my children the same thing my parents would tell me, "Do as I say, not as I do." This thought process and saying was completely wrong. I had an opportunity to do something different and break the cycle of blind obedience, however dysfunctional or wrong it was.

We have to be able to examine ourselves, see the areas that need improvement, and make the necessary adjustments to improve and be better. We can no longer continue to remain caught up in our own world, that we refuse to hear or accept truth or stop to take inventory of our moral compass. It is my responsibility to teach my children how to properly love and respect their father or any person of respect and authority in their lives.

Day Twenty-Five

February 7, 2020

Regardless of how angry I may become with my husband, I cannot react negatively toward him in front of our children. When this does occur his response is always the same, "You can't help doing what you were taught. Growing up you watched your mother yell at your father in front of you and your siblings, and now you do the same thing." However, I do not have to do the same thing. I can choose to do something different. I could change if I wanted to change, however, I chose not to change. When I look at my husband, I become angry and enraged because I have not let go of past hurt and disappointment. We have repeatedly failed each other with our lack of nonparticipation or fully committing to the maintenance of our relationship. We can no longer afford to point fingers at each other, when the issue is that we have both dropped the ball. I dropped the ball with my blatant disrespect and ensured that I did whatever I wanted to do whenever I saw fit to do so. My husband dropped the ball by idly sitting by and allowing things to just occur. No one wanted to take responsibility or be accountable for the role that they played in the process of destroying a relationship, a marriage, a family.

I fully accept and understand that because of my nature or strong personality that I will be viewed as the overpowering one dominating and manipulating anything that did occur between us. However, I fully understand that there are two sides to every coin, two sides to every story, and it takes two to make or break something. It is the responsibility of both spouses to make the decision to say, "Enough is enough, no more games. Let's commit to rectifying that which was broken and do the work to ensure that no one involved walks away cracked and bleeding, but that we walk together healed and whole."

However, I would be a boldfaced liar if I never said there weren't any happy moments or good days, because they do exist. There are days when I look at my husband and smile because he did or said something that I found amusing. Those are the days that I desire to see more of. However, it is going to take effort. I first must examine myself and work on those areas in my life that need adjustments and apply those necessary changes. It is imperative to understand that as time goes by people change, their thought process shifts, and in any relationship, there are going to be issues especially if the individuals in that particular relationship are not on the same page. My husband and I were not in sync, and I doubt if we ever really were. I recall he and I having a conversation about doing things together—we even drafted out a five-year plan. However, that plan was never manifested. Along the way on our journey, we took too many wrong turns. He went right, I went left, I took too many left turns and ended on the wrong street.

Day Twenty-Six

February 8, 2020

I can't be fake. I cannot pretend nor do I like when people are fake and pretend with me. I just encountered a fake conversation where the individual asked me how I was doing, how was my business doing, and before I could complete my sentence, the individual proceeded to share with me all of the great things happening for them and in their business. I congratulated them. I respect everyone's success and will celebrate them accordingly. However, do not ask me a question if you are not sincerely interested in what I have to say.

Everyone's on their journey of success, and who am I to be upset that a person woke up one day and decided to shift their thought process, becoming committed to achieving their goals? Celebrate the success of others, respect their process, but never compare yourself to anyone else or think too highly of yourself. Advance to each level humbly and encourage others along the way. In life we must run our own race; we cannot get caught up with what other people are doing. Celebrate the victories of others, learn from them, and continue to run your race. Don't take things personal, just continue to do the work to reach your goals, continue to run your race. Remain focused, pace yourself, and keep your eyes on your target.

Make a game plan for you to achieve your goals. Connect yourself to the right people who have already sat in the seat you are sitting in and follow through with your plan. If what you are doing is not working, then you need to make the necessary adjustments. Read more books, study what you are trying to be successful in. Your thoughts control your emotions, so become a healthy thinker and display healthy emotions. Before things can change, you first have to change your posture, change your way of thinking. The paradigm shift is a lifestyle change.

Shift your priorities and balance your life. You have to maximize your time. It's one thing to be busy, however, being productive is entirely different. Become organized and discipline yourself, because time wasted is money lost. Once time is gone you cannot gain it back. We have to make the most with the time we have. Understand and know what or who is holding you back and drop the dead weight. You can lose sight of your goals reaching back to help others who don't even want to be helped. People want you to carry them on your back and do everything for them. "If you give a hungry man a fish, you feed him for a day, but if you teach him how to fish, you feed him for a lifetime" (Lao Tsu). What does it really take to win? Understanding how to answer that question starts with your thought process and knowing which areas in your life need to change. You are already a winner. In this season you can no longer be comfortable in your uncomfortable situation. Winning is in your thought process. You first have to win in your mind.

Fulfill your divine life purpose by becoming obsessed with reaching destiny. We must understand the road we are on and take control of our lives. It is imperative to hold yourself accountable. Dress for the part, act the part, look the part until you are actually walking in the part you desire to be. Do the work until what you desire is manifested within your life. Whatever you are going to do you must do it with passion. Be willing to sacrifice something to receive something greater. We must remain consistent with doing what needs to be done to fulfill our divine life purposes.

Day Twenty-Seven

February 9, 2020

Today was a good day. God is changing the hearts of the people. God is with me, so there is no need to fear. "Then the Lord said to Jacob, 'Go back to the land of your fathers and to your relatives, and I will be with you'" (Genesis 31:3 NIV). What surprised me today was a phone call I received from my mother-in-law. She called to tell me that she shared my first project and in doing so I was invited to come and share. I was a little reluctant to agree at first. However, I was reminded of the dream I had with the numbers and various destinations and one of the destinations was New York. God is bringing me back to the place where I was done wrong, taking me back to the place where I was supposed to die. I am returning not to stay but for those same people to see me succeed. They cannot sit at the table until I get there. I was met with so much opposition. When I first arrived, I went there with open arms ready to love and they slapped my arms away. I left bitter and angry. I have been stripped of everything only to be restored, because I have sowed into the lives of so many; my seed has sustained me and my family. God's word is being manifested.

He said, "I'll make your enemies a footstool for your feet" (Psalms 110:1 NIV). I was reluctant to respond because I understand that people have hidden agendas. However, after prayer my answer was to go and allow the people to see that it is God at work, and they had nothing to do with it. God is changing the hearts of the people.

Day Twenty-Eight

February 10, 2020

What is happening in our lives is not punishment but transformation for elevation. We must come out reformed with a new thought process. How can we truly understand what someone is going through or have experienced, unless we have walked a mile in their shoes?

Day Twenty-Nine

February 11, 2020

Within these one hundred days, God has been revealing things to me through dreams and visions. I just woke up from another dream. However, my only question is, if what I'm seeing is for me to warn certain individuals in the dream or just take notation. Be still, be silent, and watch everything unfold. I prayed, asking God for interpretation, and I was led to read Habakkuk 2:2-3. "Write down the revelation and make it plain on tablets so that a herald may run with it. For the revelation awaits an appointed time; it speaks of the end and will not prove false. Though it linger, wait for it; it will certainly come and will not delay" (Habakkuk 2:2-3 NIV). In the dream I had there were three young girls. The first young girl was sad and depressed, and she accused the man in the dream of sexually abusing her. Her case was settled and dismissed. However, this girl was still depressed and never fully vindicated. People taunted her to the point that she wanted to commit suicide.

I was sitting in the bathroom in a building of a large campus, and from the window I could see the girl standing at the edge of the sidewalk, about to step off the curb and fall forward into a large puddle of water. The water was deep enough to drown herself. I opened the door and yelled at her not to do it. She stopped, looked up, and stared directly at me. I could see her eyes from where I was, which was a good distance away, almost two hundred feet. Her eyes were calling for me to help her. Someone came to grab her, and they walked toward my direction. I was still in the bathroom, but I could see them walking by. As they got closer, I could see her eyes—she was staring through me. Her eyes grabbed me and took me to another place nearby where there were two other girls in trouble. I was now standing in front of the man who was accused of abusing the first girl I saw.

I said to him, "You can have any woman, why these young girls?" He looked at me and smiled, asking me if I was jealous because they were old enough, just younger than me. I stated that I wasn't jealous, I explained to him that what he was doing was not right because they were only seventeen. His face immediately turned black, and I could hear his heart beating extremely fast. The girls came out of the room, and one of them had a black eye. I looked at them, then him and took off running with the girls. He yelled for me to come back with them. I continued to run, looking for someone I could bring them to for safety. I recalled seeing a nice woman near the bathroom I was in. I ran outside asking if anyone had seen the woman I was looking for. I was immediately directed to where she was. I found the woman in the ladies' room of the building the first girl walked out of. Her back was turned towards us. I was about to speak when she urged us to come in. We walked in, and I sat down on the toilet seat—for some reason I needed to use the bathroom again. As I was sitting on the toilet, the man chasing us came in, busting the door down. I yelled that he couldn't come in. As I was yelling, the woman walked over towards him, and he snatched her out of the bathroom. I jumped off the toilet seat and washed my hands. I told the girls we needed to get out of there. I knew we couldn't go out the front door and the drop from the window to the ground was too high. We were running out of options and needed to think fast.

I told the girls to fix the door and put the couch in the bathroom up against the door. A smoke bomb was thrown into the window. The only other way out was through the ceiling. We had to climb up and out. I had the girls get the other couch, stand it up, and remove the sliding squares from the ceiling and we climbed through. I was baffled as to why the woman was so calm when the man grabbed her. Then I realized she was his wife, and she was helping him. She was unsuspecting, so unassuming, quiet. She has been helping him keep his good name. However, we were still able to escape, and he was brought into custody, went to trial and anyone attached to him. Their reputation was ruined, and they were also investigated uncovering their mess as well.

We all have mess, waste that we eliminate that can't be flushed away—it keeps resurfacing. In the dream I was in the bathroom sitting on an open toilet in public view eliminating waste twice. However, that waste was never flushed or properly discarded. However, I was willing to help someone else get to safety, while I still had the mess not flushed away. How can you help someone else or want to help someone else and your mess is still fresh, just floating around not properly discarded? When we don't properly discard our mess, it will come back up, leaving a foul odor. Within these one hundred days everyone's mess will be uncovered in order to clear the infection. No one will be exempt, that's why we must ask God for mercy.

God is doing a clean sweep: "'I will sweep away everything from the face of the earth,' declares the LORD. 'I will sweep away both man and beast; I will sweep away the birds in the sky and the fish in the sea and the idols that cause the wicked to stumble. When I destroy all mankind on the face of the earth,' declares the LORD, 'I will stretch out my hand against Judah and against all who live in Jerusalem. I will destroy every remnant of Baal worship in this place, the very names of the idolatrous priests - those who bow down on the roofs to worship the starry host, those who bow down and swear by the LORD and who also swear by Molek, those who turn back from following the LORD and neither seek the LORD nor inquire of him'" (Zephaniah 1:2–6 NIV).

What stood out for me in the dream were the numbers three, seventeen, and twenty-nine because today is day twenty-nine. Of the three girls, two of them were age seventeen and twenty-nine—the age of the first girl is unknown. However, she was older than the other two in her twenties. We can assume that she was twenty-nine. I looked up the meaning of the numbers three, seventeen, and twenty-nine. The number three biblically represents divine wholeness, completeness, and perfection. God, himself, is described as triple, three in one whole entity. "Who is, and who was, and who is to come" (Revelation 1:4 NIV). Biblically the number three is used to signify a divine seal of completion or fulfillment of a matter. Biblically the number seventeen is a symbol of victory and perfection. The number seventeen is symbolic of self-discipline and responsibility. It is time to take responsibility over your life, becoming independent. The number seventeen also symbolizes having victory or overcoming and restoration. The number twenty-nine represents the process of living well and realizing our profound nature. These numbers may not have any real significance to anyone else but me. However, there is a message here. My interpretation of the dream was that my current situation was now coming to an end, that I will now have victory overcoming all that I had experienced. What God was doing in and through me is being perfected. I now have to take control of my life and be responsible as I travel on the journey of my life path to living well and fulfilling my divine purpose on this earth. Our lives do not belong to us, and God has a specific plan and will for all of us. "'For I know the plans I have for you,' declares the LORD, 'plans to prosper you and not to harm you, plans to give you hope and a future'" (Jeremiah 29:11 NIV).

Day Thirty

February 12, 2020

I recall my mother once telling me, "That one day your children would make you cry." Well beloved, that day finally came. Last night my child said something to me that broke my heart. I had become frustrated with my child coming home with a frown on her face, and I finally decided to pull her away from everyone else just to talk with her privately. I said that she was able to tell me what was on her heart, whatever it is, that the space we were in was a judgment free zone. Everyone needs that one person that they can confide in without judgment. Of course, we can easily say, "Cast your cares upon the Lord," however, let's be real. We are all human, and in being human you want to be able to confide in someone you can physically see and trust. Besides, God lives in me, Christ is in me, and my temple is his dwelling place. My baby was crying out for help, and I needed to figure out a way of how I could help her.

She refused, so I began to ask her questions. I said, "Do you think I will get upset?" She said, "Yes." I said, "Not today," and she began to share her heart. As I listened, I became sad because what I was hearing was hurting my heart. I allowed my child to finish

77

sharing, and after she finished, she stated that she felt better. I hugged her and told her that I loved her, that her entire family loves and cares for her and we should always feel free and comfortable enough to share our hearts with each other because we are family. I left the room and walked into the bathroom and immediately fell to the floor crying. Every parent wants their children to be safe, happy, and healthy and have all that they desire, within reason. After crying for thirty seconds too long I got up off the bathroom floor, wiped my face, walked out, and sat down on my bed. I prayed, asking God to give me strength because my pain turned into anger and frustration. However, I did not say anything to my child or displayed any anger towards her comments because I promised that I wouldn't, and I kept my word. I understand that it is important to empathize with our children and be sensitive to their needs especially during the early stages of development. However, that does not mean giving in to their every demand or desire. Children know how to play mind games and will test you to see how far they can go or get away with.

I allowed what my child said to filter through me and observed her interaction with me and the rest of her immediate family this morning. I observed what I already knew from the beginning, however valid her points were during our conversation; I understood the truth. My child is very arrogant and needs to learn how to be humble. Within these hundred days I am not walking on this journey alone. It is for my entire family to willingly participate in the transformation process and come out better and fully able to fulfill our divine purpose in life. Everyday our children will experience feelings and emotions that will flow and change, seasons change, reasons change, time changes and people change. Therefore, it is imperative for us as parents to look deeper into each situation and clearly see the needs of our children and guide them accordingly down the right path of honesty, truth, and alignment with the will of God for our lives.

Day Thirty-One

February 13, 2020

Today started out a little weird. My thoughts were clouded, I had my daily devotion. However, my mind drifted. I was able to get some things done, however, not all I wanted to get done. I have been very sensitive today and extra emotional, but not as emotional as yesterday. However, I thought about a friend and how much they helped me, and God told me to bless them and say thank you. I knew I needed the money and should save every penny or bill I can get my hands on. However, I also knew it was imperative for me to obey God. I understand that everything belongs to God, everything I have belongs to God. I am still living in a hotel with my family watching everyone around me get blessed. I had a weak moment and I questioned God.

First, I thanked God for blessing each person one by one, then I said, "When is it my turn?" No response. I then said, "Your will be done, teach me your ways, show me how to be patient without complaining." One of the fruits of the spirit is longsuffering: "But the fruit of the Spirit is love, joy, peace, longsuffering, gentleness, goodness, faith, meekness, temperance: against such there is no law. And they that are Christ's have crucified the flesh with the affections and lusts. If we live in the Spirit, let us also walk in the Spirit. Let us not be desirous of vain glory, provoking one another, envying one another" (Galatians 5:22–26 KJV). How can I be so selfish knowing that I have not fully followed every command, so I will continue to wait and trust the process. "But let patience have her perfect work, that ye may be perfect and entire, wanting nothing" (James 1:4 KJV). In obeying God, I cash-apped my friend and they texted me asking, "How did I know?" What I sent was right on time and exactly what they needed at that particular moment. All I could say was, "Amen, God knows exactly what we need and how we are going to receive it before we do."

Day Thirty-Two

February 14, 2020

Yesterday God spoke to me and said, "Go to New York." At first I said, "No" but God said, "Go." God said, "I'm bringing you back to the place where you were left for dead." "Then the Lord said to Jacob, 'Go back to the land of your fathers and to your relatives, and I will be with you'" (Genesis 31:3 NIV). God was changing the hearts of the people. I obeyed God and took the ride to New York with my family. When I go to church on Sunday, the people will see the Word of God being manifested in my life. Glory to the Lamb of God. The blue fire of God is about to flow through that church.

Day Thirty-Three

February 15, 2020

Today was a day filled with revelation. Upon arriving here, I told my husband that this would be a trip where people would sow into us, that God would change the hearts of the people and it has already started. Regardless, if they did it in secret. The people are going to pour into our lives and sow in abundance.

Day Thirty-Four

February 16, 2020

Today was a day of confirmation. I was reminded that what I have gone through was not for bad, or punishment but for my good. God allowed everything to occur for my good. The woman of God who preached today confirmed that I was supposed to be there. God showed me that the woman preaching would be the next pastor of that church. I spent time with friends and family and was reminded of the word from God spoken over my life. I am grateful to God and excited about what is about to happen, and everything is happening so fast. God can change your entire situation in an instant.

Day Thirty-Five

February 17, 2020

Today was an awe-inspiring day. People around me, within my inner circle, are being blessed and having transformative experiences. I am happy for them because I have prayed that God would bless them first before blessing me. I am already blessed. However, I know that something huge is on the horizon. Things are starting to unfold right in front of me. I knew things would start moving fast, however, I just didn't know how fast.

Day Thirty-Six

February 18, 2020

A wise person once said, "Sometimes you have to slow down to speed up" (Dan Davis). Today I took a step backward only to make a giant leap forward. Sometimes to really be done with a thing you have to ensure that you completely purge because you don't want to have any residue left over. When a thing is not fully out of your system that leftover residue can sneak up on you. If you are wondering what I am referring to, I'm talking about soul ties. I made the mistake of falling for the wrong person. For as long as I can remember, I have always caught feelings quickly and for the wrong guy. This primarily occurs and has occurred because I didn't know my value or my worth and was excited about the idea of knowing someone I was interested in was interested in me, even if it was just sex.

Even after getting married, I still didn't know my value, my worth and sought attention outside of my marriage only to find that what I searched for was cancer waiting to eat me alive. I spent most of my teen years leading into my adulthood as the sweet sister or friend. Never the girlfriend or lover, the side piece or one nightstand but never the woman anyone wanted to marry. I was always rejected by the guys or men I liked, being made to feel that I was undesirable, that I was missing something. I would question what was wrong with me that the opposite sex or at least the ones I was interested in didn't find me attractive. I knew I had a lot to offer. I can't entirely say that the opposite sex didn't find me attractive or interested, there were a few. However, I was not interested in them.

If a person male or female, is interested in you, they will make time for you. They will reach out to contact you, it will not be a one-sided love affair in your mind. I asked a question today hoping for a different response. However, I have acknowledged that my relationship with this person was going to be what it was. There will always be mutual respect but nothing more. The past is just that: the past. Reaching backward will only hinder your progress of transformation.

When I was single it was bad, however, now married and still not knowing my value, still not knowing the value of what I have. There is a disconnect. I thought I was over this person, but clearly I was not. I have been told to fast and pray to be delivered. Honey, I have come to tell you that wasn't going to work because I wasn't fully ready to let go. I was holding on to a couple of brief moments. I cried something terrible today—it was really sad. I am upset with myself because I still desired to ingest poison when the antibiotic was right in front of me. My friend called me, and I shared what happened. They understood and were inspired on how to handle their situation. When they just need to see what is in front of them.

I cannot force anyone to see what is real or what is an illusion. My friend did, however, help me to see what happened today and contributed to my growth and transformation process.

Day Thirty-Seven

February 19, 2020

I know without a shadow of doubt that God is trying to get my attention. God has been dealing with me with dreams, visions, numbers, and dates, and I look up the meaning of the numbers biblically and spiritually because there is always a message there. I took a shower this evening, and after stepping out of the shower, I saw that the mirror above the sink was fogged up. However, there were numbers written on the mirror with a finger. I knew neither my kids nor my husband were in the bathroom because the door never opened, and when I walked out of the bathroom they were sound asleep.

At first I was a little alarmed, but then I said someone has left me a message. God has left me a message, and it is important because I have never seen anything like that before. The numbers I saw written on the mirror were 114 and 19,113 was written underneath the first set of numbers. I researched the number 114 first, then the number 19 followed by the number 191 and then 13. Why did I do this? Because I felt the urge to do so. God speaks to all of us, we just have to be willing to listen.

After researching the meaning of the numbers, the message was very clear. I must, must, must remain focused and push harder to reach my goal of fulfilling my divine purpose in this life. Spiritually the number 114 means to keep your focus on manifesting your goals and aspirations. Biblically number nineteen is used as a symbol of faith. People who have faith in God will have lives full of love and peace even in the midst of turbulent times. People need faith in Jesus and also in His cross. The number nineteen represents a period of mercy before the judgment of God is manifested. I must continue to trust God and get back in alignment. The number nineteen also symbolizes that a situation or condition will soon come to an end. A new beginning is approaching, and it is imminent.

The number 113 refers to new beginnings or positive changes. Before something new comes into your life it is always necessary to close one door in order to open a new door. The number 191 symbolizes focusing on fulfilling the plan that is made for your life. I have to learn to maintain a positive attitude and belief about my future. Biblically the number thirteen is symbolic of rebellion against God and the judgment of God on such lawless behavior. True followers and believers of Christ should not fear the number thirteen. I must remain in alignment, continue to wait patiently because all difficulties in life should be taken in stride and will succeed in the end. The darkness of night is about to break into dawn. It is imperative to appreciate all the challenges and struggles and not be afraid to make the tough decisions because they will prove to be the right decision that will bring me into destiny. My future will be brighter.

Day Thirty-Eight

February 20, 2020

Today was a defining moment for me. I realized that who I cover and protect will never fully cover and protect me the same way. It is sad and unfortunate but true. We can love people, do all we can for them and not receive the same in return. No one wants to be a doormat. However, people only do what you allow. No one wants to be treated badly, used or abused. If you leave a situation and then return expecting a different result, you are only fooling yourself.

Day Thirty-Nine

February 21, 2020

I received a phone call from an associate today that was somewhat alarming. After speaking with them and making sure they were okay, I thought about something they said and reflected on what a friend had told me the other day. Their words kept repeating in my head, "Be Wise." We cannot be so desperate for love, attention, or acceptance that you allow anyone to come into your inner space. God does not make mistakes. I have realized that no matter how nice they may seem above the surface, some people are just plain crazy and will go to any length to suck you into their world of crazy. Yes, fairytales can come true, just not today.

God told me a long time ago to get out while I still had time. During my conversation with this person a question was asked. "Are you ready for your test?" Naturally I responded with, "What test?" I thought they were referring to something we had previously discussed that was work related, until they stated that my test was a test to see if they could trip me up. Satan is bold and will come straight to your face. I remained quiet and listened while this person continued to talk. I began to laugh as they really thought I would be tempted to do anything with them. I heard those same words repeating in my head again: "Be wise."

I understood exactly what they wanted from me, and I quickly apologized for giving them the wrong impression. I said, "I am not interested in taking a ride anywhere with you today or any other day." I continued to say, "Just because I may be dealing with a current issue or in need of something does not mean I'm in need of anything that you are offering." We cannot allow our situations, no matter how terrible they may seem, to cause us to become so desperate that we completely abandon our morals to fulfill that need. We must remain patient and be vigilant in doing the work that needs to be done and have faith that in time we will reap the fruits of our labor and our labor will not be in vain. A few hours later a friend reached out to me. I had offered to assist them with their situation However, I heard God speaking and said, "It's a trap, don't get tripped up." I then heard the words, "Be wise," in my head again. Fortunately I was unable to assist any further than what I had already done.

Day Forty

February 22, 2020

This morning my husband said something to me that prompted me to seriously consider and listen carefully to what he was saying. He said, "People are like weeds, and you have to pull them out from around you. You want to have strong, healthy grass." I looked at him and said, "Yes." He continued to say, "At some point you are going to have to let your friend go because they are not healthy thinkers, they are not behaving right and are all wrong for your life." He was a hundred percent correct. I know for a fact that I am moving closer to my destiny because I'm continuously being tested, one after the other, back-to-back. I must continue to watch and pray because where I'm headed not everyone can go with me.

Day Forty-One

February 23, 2020

Today started out as a good day, until I received a phone call from an old friend and a new friend. Growing up, I never really had real friends and the people I considered friends turned out to be friend-enemies, friends in disguise. Anyway, I spoke with an old childhood friend and just shared with them some things that were going on. I didn't have anything to hide and spoke with them in front of my husband. I didn't want to have a private conversation because if I can't talk on the phone in the presence of my husband then there is no need to say anything at all.

After being stripped bare, I no longer want to hide, I no longer want to pretend because if everything is not well in your life, it's not going to be well until things change. Therefore, it is not necessary to pretend. However, we must learn how to navigate through those difficult moments in our lives gracefully. I recall growing up and one of the rules of the house was, "What happens in this house, stays in this house." Meaning you must remain quiet. My mom would say to me often, "Talk to Jesus, cast your cares on the Lord." As a child, even as an adult, this saying was painful for me to adhere to because I would suffer in silence. When we suffer in silence, without properly filtering our feelings, thoughts, or emotions, a small issue can soon grow into an even bigger issue causing a multitude of unwanted problems. Therefore, I truly believe that we all need someone we can share with what is on our heart without judgment.

However, I understand that you cannot share everything with everyone because people have hidden agendas. As I continued to talk to my childhood friend, I watched the facial expression of my husband. I knew that he wanted me to hang up. I continued to talk with them because I knew that they needed encouragement not knowing fully about whatever they were facing at that present moment. As my friend began to share, I watched as the posture and facial expression of my husband changed. He was now listening to my conversation intently and began to show an expression of compassion. Sometimes in order for others to become healed and delivered we have to share our own testimonies. For we are overcomers by the word of our testimonies: "And they overcame him by the blood of the Lamb, and by the word of their testimony; and they loved not their lives unto the death" (Revelation 12:11 KJV).

When we hold things in and don't release them, what we are holding on the inside can grow into something lethal which can potentially infect the body, causing illness. Later on during the day I received a phone call from a new friend and as expected the conversation was centered around the same topic from previous conversations. I made the comment about not fully trusting the intentions of people, and my husband stated that it was time to cut my new friend loose. He stated that this person was not good for me, not good for us, and nothing they say can truly be trusted.

Day Forty-Two

February 24, 2020

Sometimes we can jump into things too quickly without having all of the information. We must be wise in all things, never be in a hurry to connect ourselves to people or make hasty decisions. Everything that glitters is not gold. What may look like gold is really gold-plated, no real value. My grandmother used to say, "You have to investigate who you plan on aligning yourself with." We should never be in a hurry to do anything without properly taking the time to do research and study. The Bible states in Philippians 4:6–8 to "be careful for nothing; but in everything by prayer and supplication with thanksgiving let your requests be made known to God, and the peace of God which passeth all understanding shall keep your hearts and minds through Christ Jesus" (KJV). We have to ask God for wisdom in all things and not feel bad about being honest with people, because if people can't accept you being honest with them then they don't deserve to be put in any category of your life.

Day Forty-Three

February 25, 2020

I remember praying one day in the basement of my parent's house, and I said to God, "Remove anyone out of my life who means no good to me, even if it's my family members." Well, some things in my life have changed, and I thought the ones closest to me would want to celebrate, however, they all have not been genuine. God is showing me the hearts of the people. Who I thought were friends really didn't care, they just wanted me to encourage and support them. Family members who I thought would automatically be there were not, and rather than say what was really on their heart, they hid it, a never-ending cycle of deception and deceit. Why do people feel the need to hide or lie to the ones they claim they love? Do they feel that their image will be distorted in the eyes of their loved ones?

I prayed to God asking God to not let me be a stumbling block to anyone, including myself. Not receiving the love and support from whom you desire is very hurtful. "He came unto his own and his own received him not" (John 1:11 KJV). I do know to the ones who knew from the beginning my worth and value and stood by me shall be blessed beyond measure, because it is God who is putting all of this together. People will not understand and will spread lies, rumors, and even some truth from the past, but God. God said I will raise you up for all the world to see. I will not be denied, and the people will see the glory of God manifested in my life.

Day Forty-Four

February 26, 2020

Faith under pressure is a trying experience. People on the outside looking in have observed my current situation and have come to the conclusion that I and my family are in distress. I have been told that because my family and I are living in a hotel we are homeless, not knowing that God told me we are going from hotel to mansion. At first I was a little unsure because we stayed with my parents for the summer against my better judgment, but my husband insisted that we go there. Needless to say, that arrangement did not work out. I have taken out loans and sold books and travel reservations and did what I could.

However, when my youngest child needed to be picked up today, and I was unable to pick her up because I no longer had a vehicle and her father was unavailable, I had to call on my parents. I love my parents, however, I knew that it would be an issue because I would be disrupting whatever plan they had which was really nothing. However, I knew that my father would have a lot to say. Upon arriving at our dwelling place my father proceeded to tell me with an attitude that I needed to drop my pursuit of working for myself and get a job. Medically I am currently unable to work and function at full capacity. We have fallen on hard times; we didn't have enough money to sustain our household and financially we need help. My situation can change in an instant, and my family has the resources and means to change it. However, no one has offered, nor should I expect them to do so, and when I do ask for financial assistance, I'm turned down or plagued with a series of questions as to why and for what reason. I found those questions very interesting because when I am called upon for financial assistance, I don't ask questions. I just do, not expecting anything in return because God has blessed me and my family to be in a position to help, especially my family members. However, I understand that you cannot rely on family or anyone else, only God.

Day Forty-Five

February 27, 2020

It is imperative to understand that life will always happen, and things are going to occur. I lost focus. Rather than trusting God fully, I became reactionary and put myself in an even deeper hole. When you are reactionary, you are only focusing on the current situation. Rather than being proactive and creating a plan to address the issue and ensure that you never return to this place again. I have been disappointed that people whom I love and say they love me have not bothered to reach out and attempt to assist me out of this hole that I voluntarily put myself in. I attempted to help myself and only made things worse. Rather than trusting God fully, I became reactionary. I looked to my husband for guidance asking him how we were going to come out of this pit.

We had money, I made plenty of money, however, I did not save money and ignored my husband's plea of concern about our financial situation and said he was too fearful and didn't trust God. I was ignorant about the value of money, and I was ignorant about the value of what I had. I didn't just mismanage my finances, I mismanaged everything God had placed in my hand because I did not understand the value of what was in my possession and did not properly maintain or do the work to preserve or enhance what I had. Our faith will always be tested, unexpected events within life will always occur. However, we must always remain wise, never losing sight of what is more important.

Day Forty-Six

February 28, 2020

I stated earlier that I was thrust into this journey, this transformation process due to a series of traumatic events. One of those events was so traumatic that I barely have a recollection of what transpired. Although I cannot recall everything, I do recall the beginning and the end. However, the middle is missing, and since that night I have been having visions and glimpses of what transpired. I shared with a friend what I recalled from that night because I felt safe with them. We allow each other a space to share or vent without judgment. However, their response threw me off because I felt like I was being judged, not realizing that they understood clearly what occurred and wanted to spare me the emotional turmoil of knowing the truth. They suggested that it was best for me to leave the past where it was: in the past. However, I believe that there is a reason why this event that occurred in my life is now resurfacing. On this particular night in the early stages of my adult life, I tried something new. It was my first experience, and I trusted the person that I was with because we were talking and developing an intimate relationship, however, I was quick to trust someone I barely knew.

My poor decision-making has come with many consequences and negative repercussions. I put my life in the hands of a stranger because I liked them and enjoyed the attention that I received from them and the entire time this person had a hidden agenda. While in college I met a man. I thought he was a nice guy because we had originally met in church, and he played the organ. He was a friend of a friend, and our families were familiar with each other. I was intrigued by him and not used to receiving a lot of attention from the opposite sex, especially by someone I was also interested in. Therefore, because I did not know my worth, my value, it did not matter that this man had a secret life outside of church. All I saw was the most talented and finest man in the church was interested in me, not realizing that I was another number, a new little lamb ripe for slaughter.

I wanted this man, enjoyed his company, and anytime he came on campus to visit me, people would stop and stare or pull me to the side asking me, "How did you get him?" Some people were even bold enough to comment in front of us that he was fine, and if I didn't satisfy him, they would be willing. When we heard comments like that, we would both smile and laugh. It felt good to see that someone else wanted what I had or was envious. I felt validated being around him or seen with him. I wasn't ugly or undesirable, I was no longer in the friend zone or viewed as the sweet sister type or a reminder of someone's auntie. However, I soon found out that everything that glitters is not gold, not even gold-plated.

One night my newfound love interest came over to visit after selling his products. I never judged his occupational choices, and he liked that about me. I never judged him, and I was sweet and nice, maybe even a little too nice. We had been alone together before, and we were intimate with each other before, so I knew why he was coming over. However, this night was a little different because he said he had something for me. Like every encounter, he would knock on the door, I would greet him with a smile and a kiss. He would pick me up and straddle me on his lap. This man was fine, chocolate mocha, tall and strong. Everything on him was big; he had a lot to give and at times it was a little too much. However, on this particular night he said that he wanted me to try something different, but he wasn't sure if I could handle it.

I climbed off his lap and sat down on the bed next to him. I asked what he had in mind, and he asked me if I ever smoked before. I told him I have never smoked cigarettes or weed. He suggested I should try it. I told him I had some reservations about drugs because I have had family members who died of an overdose and who are still struggling with drug addictions. Naturally he said he understood and that what he had was an herb and it was natural. I watched as he smoked, he looked at me and handed the joint to me. I put it in my mouth as he guided me on how to smoke it, inhale and release. That was the first and last time I would smoke. I passed the joint back to him and laid down. He said, "Yeah, you feeling good right?" I said, "Yeah, nice and relaxed."

I should have known whatever he had was potent because he was a pharmaceutical salesman. He knew exactly what he was doing. I knew we were going to have sex; I just didn't understand why he would want to get me high to do so. When I awoke the next day, I was naked, and this man was laying in my bed with a stupid grin on his face. I tried to get up and could not move. My entire body hurt. From head to toe, every part of my body hurt. I looked at him and said, "What happened? Why does my body hurt?" His response was, "Yo, mama, you were wildin." I said, "That does not explain why I'm in pain." I remember asking if there was someone else there and he smiled and said, "Nah, that was all you, woo girl you really enjoyed yourself." I just laid there with no recollection as to what happened after taking one hit and the only thing this man could say was "Yo."

We continued to see each other for a few more weeks until I called to tell him that I thought I was pregnant. He immediately said it wasn't his and hung up the phone. He immediately called me back and told me to get rid of it, that he already had five kids and didn't need anymore, that he was about to get married. He said, "What am I supposed to tell my girl?" I was completely speechless. I disconnected the call and reached out to his relative who pretty much raised him because his mother was no longer living. She asked me if I went to the doctor. I indeed went to the doctor and had every test done. I was not pregnant, nor had I contracted any diseases. She simply said to me, "Baby, you are going to be okay. Thank God you didn't come out with anything you couldn't get rid of. Forget him and move on." Which brings me back to the statement, "Let the past stay where it is." However, I was able to share with another friend and they shared with me, and in sharing I was able to see that we had similar stories of rejection, pain, and not knowing our self-worth.

I was an easy target, and this man knew it. I was prey to the predator, and it is a powerful and strong person who realizes that they were prey and finally decides to say, "No more. I am valuable, I am worth more than this." Therefore, I say uhuru to that king and queen who realizes their self-worth, takes notice of what needs to be corrected in their life, and takes the necessary steps to make those corrections. There are so many people in the world who never heal from their experiences. I understand what was meant about leaving the past behind. However, until people heal, they will never be able to let go. They will always remember. However, once they finally heal, they will be able to move forward letting go. We cannot put a time limit on anyone's healing process; however, we must willingly complete the process. During these one hundred days it is all about going through and completing the transformation process. Completion of the process is critical, so we may not receive what we desire or what we so desperately pray for until we complete the process. "An incomplete process produces an incomplete product" (Dr. Todd M. Hall, Sr.).

Day Forty-Seven

February 29, 2020

Sometimes we can overshare, confiding in the wrong people. We must be careful with who we share with and how much we share. I know it is our human nature to want to connect with people and share what is on our hearts because at times what we are carrying is too heavy to bear. People are always waiting, searching for whatever they can find to pull you down or even destroy you. The Bible states in 1 Peter 5:7, "casting all your cares upon him, for he careth for you" (KJV). Things are definitely shifting, changing. I must remain wise with every decision that I make moving forward.

Day Forty-Eight

March 1, 2020

Today was a day filled with unexpected blessings. I really need to just trust God completely. When I tried to do things on my own it didn't work. When God tells you He got you, don't worry. Trust that God has you, because when you least expect it, that's when things change around you. When you change your behavior and your thought process, you become healthy in your thinking. You will see the changes and the transformation starts to take place.

Day Forty-Nine

March 2, 2020

It will be in God's time; you can't hurry anything. I sent out a prayer request the other day and immediately, my child started feeling better. I had laid hands on her, prayed over her, but when two or three coming together touching and agreeing, Jesus said, "For where two or three are gathered together in my name, there am I in the midst of them" (Matthew 18:20 KJV). "Again I say unto you, that if two of you shall agree on earth as touching anything that they shall ask it shall be done for them of my father which is in heaven" (Matthew 18:19 KJV). I took my child to the doctor so that she could return to school with a note from the doctor. They tested for COVID-19, the flu, strep, everything. The doctor walked in and said she doesn't have COVID-19, no fever, no flu, no strep. He said that he couldn't see anything wrong with her and didn't know why she was still coughing. He said, "Whatever you are doing, keep doing it, because she is perfectly healthy." Glory to the Lamb of God, fasting, praying, laying of hands and cod liver oil works! You can't tell me my God is not real.

Day Fifty

March 3, 2020

I was praying last night, just really having a conversation with God. I said to God that I was tired of being in my current situation and I was ready for things to change for the better, asking God when and how much longer this cycle must continue. This morning after completing my morning devotional, a message came through on my cell phone and it read, "God has perfect timing, never early, never late, it takes a little patience and faith but it's worth the wait." My response was, "Amen." I received a phone call from a friend today, and they said something that reminded me of something my youngest child shared with me.

My little one shared with me a vision that flashed before her eyes. The vision was that we were in a huge house, and the interior of the house was pink and gold. Everyone's bed had their initials engraved in gold on the headboard. I agreed with her and said, "Amen." I immediately thought about a vision I had about my house, a family compound, actually, and on the outside gate my initials were on the front of the gate engraved in gold. The family house was enormous, white with pillars trimmed in gold and a carport, trees, and grass and so much land it was a beautiful sight to behold. However, when my friend on the phone said, "Barbie" and how Barbie had everything and everything was pink, gold, and fancy, they continued by saying, "Everything you write down and say you will have." I received that word and believed God, that we are going from hotel to mansion, nothing but the best.

My current situation is not pleasant and looks like it has no end, but everything has a beginning and an ending. Therefore, this season of not enough and behind or negative accounts has reached its ending. However, I must wait because I don't want to make the mistake of touching something too early, canceling out my future, or having to start all over again. It will take the hand and mercy of God to fix what you tried to do or have before time. You will end up destroying yourself in the process reaching for something before its time, only to watch it end up in the hands of someone else who was patient enough to wait to complete the process and know exactly how to properly care for what God has placed in their hands.

Day Fifty-One

March 4, 2020

Today was a day of unexpected blessings. I was talking to God earlier this morning, just telling God what I needed. Not long after our conversation, I received two checks in the mail dated for January 23, 2020. Had I received the checks on or around January twenty-third, I would not have what I needed for today. God has what we need already waiting for us, and he is waiting for us to talk with Him and trust Him, and He will release what is for us at the exact moment that it is needed. It's not always when we want it, however, it is when we need it. "But my God shall supply all your need according to His riches in glory by Christ Jesus" (Philippians 4:19 KJV).

Day Fifty-Two

March 5, 2020

This morning I received an unexpected miracle. I was talking to God and right after, God supplied exactly what I needed. I started laughing; God is truly amazing. I received a message from a friend; however, the message was familiar and always the same. There is always a need, and the need is always the same. At first I felt bad for this person and even enlisted the assistance of others to help this person even after being warned to be cautious and not always lend myself or resources to the point where I have nothing left, even for myself. I have an issue with people mismanaging what was given to them and understand that I once mismanaged what was given to me or what I worked for.

I understand that people can do whatever they want with the money they earn. However, we have to put things in perspective. You need food, clothing, and shelter. We can have nice hair, shiny nails, and fresh clothes, but if we can't keep a roof over our head, there is a problem. When you see your brother or sister with a problem and offer advice or guidance, they become offended. People don't want the truth. If you tell them the truth, they become offended, and if they are "saved and sanctified," they will rebuke you. They will say things like, "If God wanted me to know something, he would tell me himself." God has already spoken through His servant or whoever he chooses to use to speak to you. If I see you about to fall, shouldn't I warn you? Are we not our brother's keeper?

How many times have we been given sound advice, how many times have we not heeded that advice? How many times have we acknowledged we were wrong and gone back to the person who gave the advice to say thank you, and then take the necessary steps to make changes? At the end of the day people have to want to change. I don't understand why people are comfortable with sitting in a mess, rather than changing.

Day Fifty-Three

March 6, 2020

I never fully realized the impact I had on the lives of others, and that stems from not knowing your worth or understanding your value and what you have to offer.

Day Fifty-Four

March 7, 2020

What is happening around us is going to continue. It started at the end of the last decade and carried over into this decade and will continue from January to January. The infection in the land must take place first. The hand of God is sweeping over the Earth. In the book of Zephaniah 1, God spoke to Zephaniah telling him of the judgment on the whole earth in the day of the Lord. "'I will sweep away everything from the face of the earth,' declares the LORD. 'I will sweep away both man and beast; I will sweep away the birds in the sky and the fish in the sea and the idols that cause the wicked to stumble. When I destroy all mankind on the face of the earth,' declares the LORD, 'I will stretch out my hand against Judah and against all who live in Jerusalem. I will destroy every remnant of Baal worship in this place, the very names of the idolatrous priests those who bow down on the roofs to worship the starry host, those who bow down and swear by the LORD and who also swear by Molek, those who turn back from following the LORD and neither seek the LORD nor inquire of him'" (Zephaniah 1:1-6 NIV).

It is during this time that no one will be exempt. "Be silent before the Sovereign LORD, for the day of the LORD is near. The LORD has prepared a sacrifice; he has consecrated those he has invited. On the day of the LORD'S sacrifice I will punish the officials and the king's sons and all those clad in foreign clothes. On that day I will punish all who avoid stepping on the threshold, who fill the temple of their gods with violence and deceit. 'On that day,' declares the LORD, 'a cry will go up from the Fish Gate, wailing from the New Quarter, and a loud crash from the hills. Wail you who live in the market district; all your merchants will be wiped out, all who trade with silver will be destroyed. At that time I will search Jerusalem with lamps and punish those who are complacent, who are like wine left on its dregs, who think, "The LORD will do nothing, either good or bad." Their wealth will be plundered, their houses demolished. Though they build houses, they will not live in them; though they plant vineyards, they will not drink the wine.' The great day of the LORD is near - near and coming quickly. The cry on the day of the LORD is bitter; the Mighty Warrior shouts his battle cry. That day will be a day of wrath, a day of distress and anguish, a day of trouble and ruin, a day of darkness and gloom, a day of clouds and blackness, a day of trumpet and battle cry against the fortified cities and against the corner towers. 'I will bring such distress on all people that they will grope about like those who are blind, because they have sinned against the LORD. Their blood will be poured out like dust and their entrails like dung. Neither their silver nor their gold will be able to save them on the day of the LORD'S wrath.' In the fire of his jealousy the whole earth will be consumed, for he will make a sudden end of all who live on the earth" (Zephaniah 1:7–18 NIV). God is passing judgment on the whole earth, rich and poor, and there is no amount of money that can save you. We must repent and get back into alignment with the will of God.

Day Fifty-Five

March 8, 2020

In spite of the calamity happening around us, God's remnant shall not lack; we will even appear to be thriving in the midst of a bad situation. These things must occur to cleanse the earth of the infection, and it first starts with the church. We all have to be willing to change or God will force us to change. Even after all of this, the plague, hurricanes, earthquakes, tornados, fires, floods, people still refuse to change.

Day Fifty-Six

March 9, 2020

God said to me to get out while I still had time. That message was not only for me but those whose lives God has placed me in. We must fully repent and completely turn away from sin. Sin is pleasurable only for a season, for there is a way that appears to be right, but it only leads to death. "There is a way which seemeth right unto a man, but the end thereof are the ways of death" (Proverbs 14:12 KJV).

Day Fifty-Seven

March 10, 2020

I woke up this morning and the news was on. They were talking about the coronavirus and how there was a shortage of hand sanitizer and Lysol. Which is true—I walked to the local store and drugstore last night and could barely find water. As I was watching the television something flashed across the screen blocking the morning news. It was a vision of a news report of the Me Too movement infecting the church. I saw thousands of women and men coming forward claiming that pastor after pastor, famous preachers have raped and made exchanges with them with money and sex. It was a really bad scandal, and someone close to my heart was named as one of the attackers of these people and participated in various sex acts and exchanges. I prayed, and not long after, I received a phone call from a woman of God, and she shared with me what God showed her concerning a person that I cared so dearly for.

The woman of God said that God showed her that this person was my assignment, and God sent me to warn him, to help him, that I must pray for him because he has not fully repented and not all the way out of it. That the man of God continues to sin and has been sinning so long and believes that because God has not punished him it is okay. She urged me to pray for the man of God and stay away. However, God is not pleased and is about to make judgment on him. I am not having these dreams and visions by accident. The Me Too movement is about to hit the church, starting with him. There are going to be many that come forward saying, "Me Too." After sharing my vision with the woman of God, I was urged again to pray for God's servant, that God does not take him all the way out.

Day Fifty-Eight

March 11, 2020

People have become very fearful. Professional sports teams are canceling seasons. People have been flooding my inbox, suggesting I should cancel my event because of the coronavirus. However, when Apostle Vonsheila Floyd (VPFloyd Ministries) said to me, "Go, because God has my blessing waiting for me." Prior to her saying this, I had just finished listening to Dr. Todd M. Hall, Sr. (the Shabach Church, Apopka FL) preaching a sermon where he said, "Even if you have to go by yourself, don't mess this up." Don't mess up your blessing by not showing up, by not being in position. Watch and see what God is about to do for you.

Day Fifty-Nine

March 12, 2020

More text messages, and even more phone calls. My response is always the same: "God, I trust you, God is a keeper." When you are met with much opposition and doubt, that only means you are that much closer to where you need to be. God has a purpose and a plan just for you. Glory to the Lamb of God.

Day Sixty

March 13, 2020

Today was a day of unexpected blessings. What can I say about Brooklyn? The world is experiencing a crisis, people are dying, falling ill, and unsure as to what to do. However, when I took a trip to Brooklyn today and observed the behavior of the people and how they carried on with their day without a care in the world, because they understood that despite what may be happening around you, life still has to continue. We have to remain focused as well as aware of what is happening around you. It's called common sense. I always wash my hands, I never touch my face with my fingers until washing my hands and I rarely talk to people anyway. No one really knows what this virus is or what its capabilities are, but I will remain cautious and refuse to live in fear.

If we claim to be baptized believers in Christ who claim to trust God and have faith but are fearful to live their lives normally, they can look at the people of Brooklyn: fearless. I don't know who is saved and who is not saved doesn't matter. What I observed was that you have to have something on the inside, a sheer will to live and survive, having faith that everything will be alright. Just automatically knowing you are going to be okay, never backing down, never giving up. I enjoyed my short stay in Brooklyn and just observing the people. It's not about not caring or not being prepared, it's the confidence in knowing and believing that everything will be okay even in the midst of tragedy. "For God hath not given us the spirit of fear; but of power, and love, and of a sound mind" (2 Timothy 1:7 KJV). If I listened to the fears of others, I would have missed my blessing. God has blessed me and my family, and it will be continuous. From this day forward, we shall not lack and will be living in increase and overflow.

Day Sixty-One

March 14, 2020

I am so glad I came to New York this weekend. Had I stayed home I would have missed my blessing. God was setting me up for my miracle. The day started off a little stressful. I was excited and nervous all at the same time. Today was the debut and launch of my business. Prior to launching my business or even reaching my destination, I was receiving a flood of text messages and phone calls of fearful people worried and concerned and wanting me to cancel. However, on this journey I have and must continue to listen to the voice of God. In doing so, the launch of my business was successful. Of course there were some spectators and haters, looking to see if I would fail. I already know that this day was ordained and orchestrated by God.

Prior to completing the set-up of my event, my husband and I prayed together in the car. I told him we needed to pray because I was not calm and needed to calm my nerves. Everyone needs someone in their life who can help to keep them balanced or leveled. As he began to pray, I just started to thank God and then I went up and in, crying out to God in thanksgiving and in doing so,

I heard God say, "It's over." From this day forward, forward motion, onward and upward. God is about to take me from glory to glory. My family will be set up for success, in every area of our lives.

Day Sixty-Two

March 15, 2020

God said that my days of suffering are over, and I'm putting everything in your hand. Your days of suffering are over, beloved, and God is putting everything in your hand. Glory to the Lamb of God.

Day Sixty-Three

March 16, 2020

This COVID-19 will lift, there will be miracles, signs and wonders, cancer and other diseases will be miraculously gone. Unexplained miracles will occur. However, people will go back to business as usual, still not repenting and fully turning away from sin, and because of this there will be another attack amongst the people and the second state will be worse than the first.

Day Sixty-Four

March 17, 2020

Today I had a moment of déjà vu. I was walking down the street, and the scene before me looked very familiar. I continued to walk, and as I turned the corner, I could see my current situation getting better. The day of dawn is breaking, and God is about to blow my mind completely and I can't mess this up. Within these one hundred days you will have to be a willing participant of the transformation process or God will force you to change. Woe unto you if God has to force you to change. In Zechariah 1:2–6, God is displeased, and He is calling us to return back to him. "Therefore say thou unto them, Thus saith the LORD of hosts; Turn ye unto me, saith the LORD of hosts, and I will turn unto you, saith the LORD of hosts" (Zechariah 1:3 KJV).

Day Sixty-Five

March 18, 2020

Today I went to take care of a few things and walked outside to get my daily steps in. However, as I was returning from my walk, I started to feel achy within my body. I was feeling ill. When I got back inside, I was a little concerned because of the COVID-19 that was going around. I had chills and a headache, no fever, but my stomach was a little queasy. I asked my friend to pray for me. I was reluctant to go to the doctor because I no longer had medical insurance. However, my friend stated that I should still be able to be seen without it. I felt better after drinking my tonic, took some Tylenol, and laid down. I am still going to go to the doctor and get checked out. I just probably need more rest, stay hydrated, and eliminate waste. A lot of times we can have excess waste in our bodies that if left inside too long can cause us to become ill. I'm pausing right there on that one because that was a whole word.

Day Sixty-Six

March 19, 2020

This morning I awoke feeling much like I did yesterday. I told my husband that I wasn't feeling well, and he freaked out. I told him to calm down, it is not the coronavirus. My head and stomach were bothering me. I didn't have a fever, and I wasn't having any problems with my breathing. Seeing that he was beginning to panic, I went and got my oil and anointed my head, stomach, pillow, and prayed. Sickness will not be my portion in Jesus' name. After I did all of that he then tells me his stomach was bothering him the day before and after eliminating he felt better. I looked at him and said, "See, there you go." I told him that I would go to the doctor later, just to make sure there was nothing more than an upset stomach.

I wanted him to stay home with me, but he is worried about finances and how we are going to survive. I told him that God will provide and has been providing for us. He left anyway. I was feeling better, just continuing to stay hydrated. I don't want to put too much on my stomach. I am thankful that the kids are away spending time with their grandparents, and I have time to go to the doctor, rest, and clear up whatever this is. I have been so concerned about others, making sure they are healthy and safe, that I must also ensure that I am healthy and safe. Not operating in fear but taking precaution. I will see if he comes back to take me to the doctor. In the meantime I will continue to take my tonic, vitamins, elderberry, and cod liver oil.

In the midst of this calamity happening around us, people are fearful and have completely suspended their lives. Some people are reckless and are carrying on as if nothing has changed, and then there are the select few who have faith, believing and trusting in God that all of this will be over soon. We must continue to pray and seek God. If this virus outbreak had not occurred, a lot of people would continue to sin not wanting to change or stop what they're doing. My concern is that once the virus is lifted, how long before we go back to business as usual? God is not pleased, and he will continue to sweep over the Earth until Zion repents and turns back to Him.

Day Sixty-Seven

March 20, 2020

I awoke early this morning feeling better and wanting something to eat. I told my husband that I should get screened for precautionary reasons. He said I was being paranoid, that if I was better, there was no need for me to get tested for COVID-19. I walked down to the doctor's office anyway. As I was walking, I stopped prematurely in front of a closer urgent care facility. I walked, and I was stopped at the entrance by a nurse. I told her the symptoms I was experiencing the last few days. However, she stated that because I did not have a fever or experiencing shortness in breath, there was no reason for me to get tested for COVID-19. While walking back home I called my husband to tell him what the nurse said. He said, "If you are going to trust God, trust God, but I am not taking you out there so you can catch something."

I received a word from the Lord today through the woman of God, Apostle Vonsheila Floyd (VPFloyd Ministries). She said, "Woman of God don't worry about anything, you are fine. God is about to release everything into the hands of His people." My husband and I both have to trust God more. I understand that during this time our faith is going to be tested. We are human and because we are human there will be times when fear or doubt may creep in. We must continue to pray and stay in the word. God has us and will continue to take care of his children. Ephesians 3:20 says, "Now unto him that is able to do exceeding abundantly above all that we ask or think, according to the power that worketh in us." We must continue to seek the Lord, "For our conversation is in heaven; from whence also we look for the Saviour, the Lord Jesus Christ" (Philippians 3:20 KJV).

In the midst of everything happening, God is going to raise up His remnant. Zephaniah 3:20 says, "At that time will I bring you again, even in the time that I gather you: for I will make you a name and a praise among all people of the earth, when I turn back your captivity before your eyes, saith the LORD." God is not pleased and will continue to sweep over the earth. "Egypt shall be a desolation and Edom shall be a desolate wilderness, for the violence against the children of Judah, because they have shed innocent blood in their land. But Judah shall dwell forever, and Jerusalem from generation to generation. For I will cleanse their blood that I have not cleansed: for the LORD dwelleth in Zion" (Joel 3:19–21 KJV). God said that He shall protect his children. "There shall no evil befall thee, neither shall any plague come nigh thy dwelling" (Psalm 91:10 KJV).

Be encouraged, God is about to hand the land over to his remnant. "Until the LORD have given rest unto your brethren, as well as unto you, and until they also possess the land which the LORD your God hath given them beyond Jordan: and then shall ye return every man unto his possession, which I have given you" (Deuteronomy 3:20 KJV). Exodus 3:20–22 says, "And I will stretch out my hand, and smite Egypt with all my wonders which I will do in the midst thereof: and after that he will let you go. And I will give this people favor in the sight of the Egyptians: and it shall come to pass, that, when ye go, ye shall not go empty: But every woman shall borrow of her neighbor, and of her that sojourneth in her house, jewels of silver and jewels of gold, and raiment: and ye shall put them upon your sons, and upon your daughters; and ye shall spoil the Egyptians." During these one hundred days in the midst of calamity, God's people will not come out empty-handed. We are coming out with all God has promised us. Glory to the Lamb of God.

Day Sixty-Eight

March 21, 2020

Psalm 91:10–11 says, "There shall no evil befall thee, neither shall any plague come nigh thy dwelling. For he shall give his angels charge over thee, to keep thee in all thy ways." Beloved, we are covered. Believe God.

Day Sixty-Nine

March 22, 2020

People will not believe until something happens. On August 5th, 2019, I shared with my husband, my parents, and a few people close to me that God was doing a clean sweep. The hand of God was going to sweep over the earth. Turns out that COVID-19 came out in 2019 and grew rapidly in 2020. It was just revealed to me that the president was made aware of the virus in November 2019. My father recently called me to tell me that I was right about what God showed me, and now he believes in visions and prophecy. However, prior to this phone call, he did not believe in prophets or prophecy. My father thought I was crazy to even believe in prophets, prophecy, or anyone who claims to be a prophet. I do not claim to be a prophet. I am not a prophet. However, God has decided to show me certain things or reveal things to me. I share what God has shown me with higher authority who can see more than I can or have more experience within the office of the prophetic. I also continue to study the Word of God and pray.

Day Seventy

March 23, 2020

This morning was a struggle because I was filled with a well of emotions. The reality of my current situation kicked in. Like Peter, I took my eye off Jesus and began to sink within the facts of my current situation. I thought about all the people I had helped or sowed into, and now those same people have distanced themselves or refuse to extend any form of assistance. I am forced to remind myself to trust God and walk away from anyone or anything that will distract me from focusing on my journey with God. I broke down in tears, and my husband comforted me, and he admitted that he was fearful. Yes, we are financially in trouble. However, we can no longer afford to make decisions out of fear and doubt. COVID-19 has shut so many things down. Although things look bad, God has still sustained us. We must continue to trust God and believe that things will work out for our good.

Day Seventy-One

March 24, 2020

How quickly people forget who has helped them. When you are down everyone wants to point out what you are not doing, what you should be doing. How naive for me to think anyone would be concerned about your state. I have to do what is best for me and my family. I laughed today when I spoke to a friend over the phone, and they shared with me that my family is not prepared to handle what is happening around us that I should not count on something that may never happen. I want to work and what I am currently doing to support my family financially is not yielding immediate fruit. I am so close to where I need to be, I cannot quit. When the smoke clears and this part of my journey is complete, people will say I don't know how you did it.

I will continue to trust God. When I help someone, I don't ask questions, I just help them. I am always there for others to get their rent paid, put food in their house. My situation is temporary. It's amazing to me that even in the midst of everything happening, I am okay, we're okay. My needs are met. I look at people who have more than enough and yet they are lost, fearful, uncertain about their future, and yet I have peace and take comfort in knowing that everything will be fine, it is all going to work out.

Day Seventy-Two

March 25, 2020

I received a phone call last night from the same friend who, earlier in the day, shared their feelings about my current situation, to tell me God has not forgotten about me, that I have to go through what I am experiencing so God gets the glory. I understand that, and that's why I didn't become upset when they were making their suggestions of what I should be doing. I reached out to a friend, just to check in and realized that our relationship has transformed into something pure, one of genuine respect and love. How we started doesn't matter, where we are headed, moving forward, is what matters the most. It is never how we start but how we finish. In the end, come what may, we will always be there for each other, much love indeed.

We must continue to pray one for another and if we should slip and fall, get up, repent, and keep moving forward. Our president is pushing for borders to be reopened and churches full on Easter. However, that is two weeks premature. My question is, are his intentions pure or politically motivated? Profit over people is dangerous and stepping out prematurely will seal the fate of millions of people. I want to go out and see churches full on Easter Sunday and every Sunday. If my church was open, I would be there. I want to go to the house of worship. However, until that time comes, my home has become my sanctuary. God has not forgotten about his people.

Day Seventy-Three

March 26, 2020

"Love lifted me, love lifted me, when nothing else could help love lifted me." Another person, someone I have known almost my entire life has died from the coronavirus. We are still here, beloved, healing, and deliverance is in Goshen. We are covered and protected by God.

Day Seventy-Four

March 27, 2020

I am up early this morning traveling to New York to get my babies. My family has had a lot to say about me, my spouse, our children, and our living situation. I know they don't see that we are being set up for a miracle. Our lives may not have been perfect, and we have a long list of issues. However, my husband and I both agreed that we would stay and see how the story ends. Whatever the reasons, why we got married doesn't matter. It's not even about us; God has a higher purpose for our family that He may be glorified.

Day Seventy-Five

March 28, 2020

My children are back home with me. I was listening to Bible study earlier in the week, at the Shabach Church in Apopka, Florida, on the topic of Goshen, and I told them the story of the children of God being protected by God in Goshen, from the plagues brought on by God against Egypt. "You shall live in the region of Goshen and be near me—you, your children and grandchildren, your flocks and herds and all you have. I will provide for you there, because five years of famine are still to come. Otherwise you and your household and all who belong to you will become destitute" (Genesis 45:10–11 NIV). Now they are walking around singing songs and yelling, "Goshen! We are in Goshen." I love my babies, and, yes, we are in Goshen. Glory to the Lamb of God.

Day Seventy-Six

March 29, 2020

There are many spiritual leaders saying God didn't send this disease, some say it is man-made. I even said that it was man-made for political reasons so the people in government, those in power, would be viewed as the savior of the people. However, only God has the power to allow anything to come through the earth. God showed me in a dream, August 5th, 2019, the hand of God coming out of the sky with a huge broom, sweeping over the earth. Bodies were falling under the broom, and a small remnant of people were coming out of the ground, replacing the people that were swept away. God showed me the hearts of the people. I cannot be fooled by the sly words of those who mean no good.

God is about to open heaven and pour out my blessing in the midst of calamity. We must wash our hands, repent, and come back into alignment. Glory to the Lamb of God. Wash your hands of sin. It is God calling His children to come back into alignment. Therefore, we must follow God's command: "Go, my people, enter your rooms and shut the doors behind you; hide yourselves for a little while until his wrath has passed by. See, the Lord is coming out of his dwelling to punish the people of the earth for their sins. The earth will disclose the blood shed on it; the earth will conceal its slain no longer" (Isaiah 26:20–21 NIV).

Day Seventy-Seven

March 30, 2020

"The Lord said unto my Lord, Sit thou at my right hand, until I make thine enemies thy footstool" (Psalm 110:1 KJV). The people that laughed at you, hated you, swore they would never speak to you, are now praying for you. They are wanting to talk to you and share with you. The tables are turning.

Day Seventy-Eight

March 31, 2020

At the end of the one hundred days there will be people miraculously healed from diseases, cancer, the coronavirus, diabetes—all will be gone. Those who stayed firm within their faith, completed the transformation process, realigned themselves within the will of God will bear witness of the miraculous power of God. God's remnant will be a powerful voice within the government. After this thousands upon thousands will run to the church. There won't be room to seat the people. God's remnant is about to be elevated and inherit the earth.

Day Seventy-Nine

April 1, 2020

Relief is coming. All of this will be over soon. At the end of these one hundred days the lives of millions of people will be transformed forever. However, there will be a select few who will not change at all. Woe unto them that don't change, for the wrath of God will be ever more severe upon them. This virus was only the beginning of the shifting. We must repent and realign ourselves in the will of God while we still have time. If you survived this wave of sickness and death, it was the hand of God that spared you. God is giving the earth to His remnant.

Day Eighty

April 2, 2020

God shall restore His people; Jeremiah 30 says this. This virus can be lifted by the end of the one hundred days. It can be lifted tomorrow. However, this process will continue, this wave of sickness and death will continue until the fierce anger of the Lord is fully accomplished. "The fierce anger of the Lord will not turn back until He fully accomplishes the purposes of His heart. In the days to come you will understand this" (Jeremiah 30:24 NIV). It is our disobedience that will prolong the process. I will continue to write down what God has spoken to me. I had a dream last night that confirmed what God said to me when I was praying with my friend yesterday.

While praying God spoke to me and said, "Go do the will of the father, for I have already prepared the way for you." However, it was after praying that I checked my phone this morning, and the message I received further confirmed that God was with me, that I will possess the land—just stay in position. Glory to the Lamb of God. I will share my dream at a later time. I must filter and process, pray, and seek God for further interpretation.

Day Eighty-One

April 3, 2020

My prophetic instructions were to obey God, so I will obey God. My conversation with my friend today confirmed what I knew they were thinking. In time God will reveal all things to us. With nineteen days left in this hundred-day journey I must socially and spiritually distance myself and allow God to fully continue to work on me and complete the process. Everyone needs love and I will continue to show love. These next nineteen days will be fast and furious, and there will be peace and relief coming to God's remnant. God's remnant will inherit the earth. What the enemy meant for evil, God is turning around for our good.

God is in control of all things. I just prayed and praised and thanked God for what He was about to do and has done and received a phone call telling me that I lost. All this waiting for what? I will continue to wait because God has the final say. I will not lie; I am a little discouraged. What did I do wrong? Was I not silent when I should have been silent? Did I not fully obey the command of God? Wow, God is about to do something so amazing, it is going to blow my mind. I am watching everyone around me be blessed and get what God promised them and I'm not going to receive my miracle? Oh no, I shall receive my inheritance, I shall receive my miracle. God has not forgotten about me. I will wait and obey you God.

Day Eighty-Two

April 4, 2020

On day eighty God spoke to me and told me to fast for twenty days. I was disobedient and now I must fast and pray and stay in the Word of God. I will continue to write after the hundredth day. God said in Jeremiah 33 that He will restore Judah and Israel. We must cry out to God, and He will answer. Jeremiah 33:3 says, "Call to me and I will answer you and tell you great and unsearchable things you do not know." God will tear down, then restore. Jeremiah 33:4–9 says, "For this is what the Lord, the God of Israel says about the houses of Judah that have been torn down to be used against the siege ramps and the sword in the fight with the Babylonians: 'They will be filled with the dead bodies of the people I will slay in my anger and wrath. I will hide my face from this city because of all its wickedness.' Nevertheless, I will bring health and healing to it; I will heal my people and will let them heal my people and will let them enjoy abundant peace and security. I will bring Judah and Israel back from captivity and will rebuild them as they were before. I will cleanse them from all the sin they have committed against me and will forgive all their sins of rebellion against me. Then this city will bring me renown, joy, praise and honor before all nations on earth that hear of all the good things I do for it; and they will be in awe and will tremble at the abundant prosperity and peace I provide for it."

Jeremiah 33:10-12 says, God will restore: "This is what the Lord says: 'You say about this place, "It is a desolate waste, without people or animals." Yet in the towns of Judah and the streets of Jerusalem that are deserted, inhabited by neither people nor animals, there will be heard once more the sounds of joy and gladness, the voices of bride and bridegroom, and the voices of those who bring thank offerings to the house of the Lord, saying, 'Give thanks to the Lord Almighty, for the Lord is good; his love endures forever.' For I will restore the fortunes of the land as they were before; says the Lord.'" God, I need you. Rescue me and my family. I don't have anything left; my life is completely in your hands. My accounts are negative, I have taken out loans and cash advances. I have mismanaged everything you gave me. I was immature, so now God I come to you laying everything before you. Asking you, Father, to forgive me, have mercy on me. Have mercy on your people; we cannot survive without you. I am nothing without you, forgive me, Abba, please. Thank you for your grace, thank you for your mercy. God, show me what I am to do. I made a complete mess over everything. It's in you, Father, that I put my trust. You lead, God, and I will follow.

Day Eighty-Three

April 5, 2020

Today is the second day of my fast. Yesterday was a beautiful day with my family. I told my husband we must elevate our faith. We prayed together; my husband was so excited. However, after we said that we would trust God, the car started to leak fluid. My husband became upset and went into panic mode. He called his friend several times who lives four hundred miles away so he cannot physically help him. He called me to come downstairs so I could help him take a video. I told him not to worry, got dressed, and went downstairs. He showed me where the problem was, but I really couldn't see anything. I assisted him with creating a video so that he could send it to his friend.

I told my husband not to worry, that God has what we need before we even need it. He then told me that he met a man the other day and gave him a ride because his car broke down and the man shared with him that he had a relative that is a mechanic, and he gave my husband his business card. I said, "See God already prepared what you needed before you needed it." I told my husband that I was going to walk down to the store and come back. He asked me to hurry back because he might need me. I wasn't sure how much more help I would have been. However, I left quickly to come back to be with him. As I walked to the store, I approached a man who was outside an apartment complex tending to the landscaping of the property. I said good morning to him, and he replied, "Good morning, and how are you?" I stated that I was well and told him to continue to stay safe and well. He told me to do the same.

Normally when I speak to people of varying ethnicities, my experience has not always been very positive or pleasant, and I am usually left walking away feeling unmotivated to even engage with people who identify with other ethnicities, especially males. However, since the COVID-19 pandemic, people of other ethnicities and decent are now speaking and are quite friendly. People that would not normally speak to each other are now speaking. Some of you reading this may be shocked to even think that such things occur. However, there are many of you reading this and completely understand the place I am writing this from. It should not take calamity or a major crisis or disaster to bring people closer together or close enough to initiate and have a general friendly conversation and show some form of care for another human being.

On my way back from the store, I was approaching the man that was landscaping. I heard God say to pray for him. I began to silently pray for him, but I knew exactly what God meant. I quickly hurried past the man in efforts to avoid any further contact with him, when he said, "Have a good day." I stopped and said, "You too, and God bless you." I could feel that the man wanted something more, a conversation, but definitely something more. However, I turned around and kept walking. That was another missed opportunity to share with someone about Jesus, or just have a casual conversation. God have mercy on me, on us who dismiss opportunities to share with others. I walked back to my husband and saw that God had sent him help. He was calling on a friend hundreds of miles away. However, I always say God knows what we need before we need it. Turns out this person was also a White man and someone he helped earlier in the week with car trouble.

I said hello to the gentleman and thanked him for assisting my husband. I told my husband that I was going upstairs to check on the kids. The man stayed with my husband and gave him a ride to the auto parts store to pick up what he needed for the car. He even paid for it and told my husband to make sure he has the correct stuff when he goes to have the oil changed. After my husband shared his story with me, we got together as a family and read the Bible. I began to read as they listened to me become excited over the Word of God. I was reading Exodus 3:21–22. When the children of Israel leave Egypt, they will not leave empty-handed. "And I will make the Egyptians favorably disposed toward this people, so that when you leave you will not go empty-handed. Every woman is to ask her neighbor and any woman living in her house for articles of silver and gold and for clothing, which you will put on your sons and daughters. And so you will plunder the Egyptians" (Exodus 3:21–22 NIV). I read Jeremiah 30:24: "The fierce anger of the Lord will not turn back until he fully accomplishes the purposes of his heart. In days to come you will understand this." Then I read Jeremiah 33, God's promise of restoration. The more I continued to read the more I became excited. I read Romans 12:17–19, which says God's wrath will avenge His people. "Do not repay anyone evil for evil. Be careful to do what is right in the eyes of everyone. If it is possible, as far as it depends on you, live at peace with everyone. Do not take revenge, my dear friends, but leave room for God's wrath, for it is written: 'It is mine to avenge; I will repay,' says the Lord."

Shortly after sharing the Word with my husband and children, I received a message from God's servant. I shared with him what was on my heart, and he told me not to worry, that God will restore. I shall be restored. I said, "Amen, glory to the Lamb of God." I will continue to trust God. It makes my heart glad that even in the midst of COVID-19 and social distancing, God's house is still open. Goshen is still thriving; there is no lack, for there is safety in Goshen. The time now is 10:35 a.m. and I am watching the Shabach Church in Apopka, Florida, and the church is filling and will be full. The walls of this church will swell and expand because God's servant has not walked in fear. My family and I will continue to worship together with God's people because we reside in Goshen. We must continue to elevate our faith. At 1:00 p.m. today we will worship over the phone with TrueVine Full Gospel Baptist Church in Manassas, Virginia. Our worship must be pure and genuine unto God. We can no longer afford to offer up to God vain repetition. We have to elevate our worship, our praise, our faith. God requires so much more from us.

Day Eighty-Four

April 6, 2020

Thousands of people will die because of stupidity. However, millions more will die from medical genocide. Doctors are selective in who can be treated and mainly focus on the most severe COVID-19 cases or those they deem important enough to save. My sister-in-law is recovering from cancer, however, when we went to pick up our children, she was having pain in her feet and hands. Her doctor treated her via video conference. Her pain and condition has gotten worse, and she is now in the emergency room. If the hospital fails to treat her condition as an emergency, she could become deathly ill. God have mercy on us when man decides who lives and who dies.

Day Eighty-Five

April 7, 2020

I have not been the best wife or the greatest role model for my family. However, I have been able to reflect on these last eighty-five days, and I am loving what I am seeing. Every day I can see transformation taking place. God is definitely doing a new thing.

Day Eighty-Six

April 8, 2020

God is calling for us to repent. "Gather together, gather yourselves together, you shameful nation, before the decree takes effect and that day passes like windblown chaff, before the LORD'S fierce anger comes upon you, before the day of the LORD'S wrath comes upon you. Seek the LORD, all you humble of the land, you who do what he commands. Seek righteousness, seek humility; perhaps you will be sheltered on the day of the LORD'S anger" (Zephaniah 2:1–3 NIV). God will continue to sweep over the earth. In Zephaniah 1, God passes judgment on the whole earth in the day of the Lord. "'I will sweep away everything from the face of the earth,' declares the LORD. "'I will sweep away both man and beast; I will sweep away the birds in the sky and the fish in the sea and the idols that cause the wicked to stumble. When I destroy all mankind on the face of the earth,'" declares the LORD, "'I will stretch out my hand against Judah and against all who live in Jerusalem. I will destroy every remnant of Baal worship in this place, the very names of the idolatrous priests those who bow down on the roofs to worship the starry host, those who bow down and swear by the LORD and who also swear by Molek, those who turn back from following the LORD and neither seek the LORD nor inquire of him'" (Zephaniah 1:2-6 NIV). "Be silent before the Sovereign LORD, for the day of the LORD is near. The LORD has prepared a sacrifice; he has consecrated those he has invited. On the day of the LORD'S sacrifice I will punish the officials and the king's sons and all those clad in foreign clothes. On that day I will punish all who avoid stepping on the threshold, who fill the temple of their gods with violence and deceit. 'On that day,' declares the LORD, 'a cry will go up from the Fish Gate, wailing from the New Quarter, and a loud crash from the hills. Wail you who live in the market district; all your merchants will be wiped out, all who trade with silver will be destroyed. At that time I will search Jerusalem with lamps and punish those who are complacent, who are like wine left on its dregs, who think, "The LORD will do nothing, either good or bad." Their wealth will be plundered, their houses demolished. Though they build houses, they will not live in them; though they plant vineyards, they will not drink the wine.' The great day of the LORD is near—near and coming quickly. The cry on the day of the LORD is bitter; the Mighty Warrior shouts his battle cry. That day will be a day of wrath, a day of distress and anguish, a day of trouble and ruin, a day of darkness and gloom, a day of clouds and blackness, a day of trumpet and battle cry against the fortified cities and against the corner towers. 'I will bring such distress on all people that they will grope about like those who are blind, because they have sinned against the LORD. Their blood will be poured out like dust and their entrails like dung. Neither their silver nor their gold will be able to save them on the day of the LORD'S wrath.' In the fire of his jealousy the whole earth will be consumed, for he will make a sudden end of all who live on the earth" (Zephaniah 1:7-18 NIV).

All this death, all this disease and destruction and yet there are still those who will not believe, those who are still unrepentant. "'I have destroyed nations; their strongholds are demolished. I have left their streets deserted, with no one passing through. Their cities are laid waste; they are deserted and empty. Of Jerusalem I thought, "Surely you will fear me and accept correction!" Then their place of refuge would not be destroyed, nor all my punishments come upon her. But they were still eager to act corruptly in all they did. Therefore wait for me,' declares the LORD, 'for the day I will stand up to testify. I have decided to assemble the nations, to gather the kingdoms and to pour out my wrath on them - all my fierce anger. The whole world will be consumed by the fire of my jealous anger'" (Zephaniah 3:6-8 NIV).

Day Eighty-Seven

April 9, 2020

When I saw the hand of God sweeping over the earth in my dream, I had no idea as to what exactly would occur or how severe it would be. I understood that we needed to realign ourselves with the will of God and repent. The Word of God is true and is being manifested through the earth. After COVID-19 God is not done, because after God swept over the earth in my dream, there was only a small remnant that came up behind the millions of people that were swept away. For every two to three million people, there were only three to four people that sprung up from the ground, behind the bodies being swept away. There were only a handful of people left on the earth. God told me that no one was exempt from His wrath; we must get right and stay right. "Therefore, the LORD, the LORD Almighty, the Mighty One of Israel, declares: 'Ah! I will vent my wrath on my foes and avenge myself on my enemies. I will turn my hand against you; I will thoroughly purge away your dross and remove all your impurities. I will restore your leaders as in the days of old, your rulers as at the beginning. Afterward you will be called the City of Righteousness, the Faithful City.' Zion will be delivered with justice, her penitent ones with righteousness. But rebels and sinners will both be broken, and those who forsake the LORD will perish. 'You will be ashamed because of the sacred oaks in which you have delighted; you will be disgraced because of the gardens that you have chosen. You will be like an oak with fading leaves, like a garden without water. The mighty man will become tinder and his work a spark; both will burn together, with no one to quench the fire'" (Isaiah 1:24–31).

Day Eighty-Eight

April 10, 2020

We have to be stripped bare in order to be restored. The earth is being stripped bare. I stated earlier there were a series of events that occurred a decade ago in my life that thrusted me into this transformation process. However, it was in August 2016 that God showed me in a vision all I was going to lose and could lose if I continued to be disobedient. I had forgotten how I was blessed and who blessed me and brought me out of my state of bondage, much like the children of Israel forgot God delivered them out of Egypt. "Remember this and never forget how you aroused the anger of the LORD your God in the wilderness. From the day you left Egypt until you arrived here, you have been rebellious against the LORD. At Horeb you aroused the LORD'S wrath so that he was angry enough to destroy you." (Deuteronomy 9:7–8 NIV).

God showed me in my vision that I would lose my job, my home, and my car. God even showed me that I would lose my husband and children. However, I did not have to lose my family if I remained obedient. When I lost my job in April 2018, I thought I was being punished for sins I committed. It wasn't until I sought the face of God, that God revealed to me that He was stripping me bare in order to restore me. So, when I lost my home in November 2018 and then my car in November 2019, I was not upset. However, when my father said to me, "You lost your car, you just received bad news," I began to worship and praise God, thankful because God showed me that I was about to be restored, that I would receive greater. My time living with my family in hotels was for me and my family to become closer together in God, for us to learn how to properly love and care for each other, and come together in prayer and thanksgiving, worshiping God together. God is calling for his children to return to Him. God is going to strip us in order to restore us, so when we come out of this, we come out better knowing how to properly love and care for one another. Glory to the Lamb of God! We will come out of quarantine knowing for real who God is. "'This is the covenant I will make with the people of Israel after that time,' declares the LORD. 'I will put my law in their minds and write it on their hearts. I will be their God, and they will be my people, No longer will they teach their neighbor, or say to one another, "Know the LORD," because they will all know me, from the least of them to the greatest,' declares the LORD. 'For I will forgive their wickedness and will remember their sins no more'" (Jeremiah 31:33–34 NIV).

Day Eighty-Nine

April 11, 2020

I said before during these one hundred days there will be many miracles even in the midst of calamity. I received a phone call today from a friend, another family that I have been praying for. I had asked God to bless them before blessing me, and God did it. My friend called to tell me that they just moved into a six-bedroom house. They didn't have the down payment; however, they prayed and fasted together, and God provided what they needed. It was money that was already theirs and a little extra was added on top of it. God knows just what we need before we need it. Had they received the money beforehand it would have gone towards something else.

They were able to close on the house and move in five days before their scheduled time. I laughed and cried, at the same time rejoicing with my friend, and we both said at the same time that I was next. My family was next to be blessed. Glory to the Lamb of God. As they continued to testify about the wondrous power of God, I began to praise and thank God for what He had done and what He was about to do. Even in this pandemic, God's remnant shall inherit the earth. Obey God and watch what happens. My friend said, "After all of this, can't nobody tell me that God isn't real." When we willingly participate in the transformation process God will show you His power. God's word will not come back void.

Day Ninety

April 12, 2020

Today is Resurrection Sunday, but some people say Easter. However, for me and most Christians it's Resurrection Sunday, the day Christ has risen from the grave. It's my prayer that the pandemic is over soon, because Christ rose from the grave conquering death. "Then the end will come, when he hands over the kingdom to God the Father after he has destroyed all dominion, authority and power. For he must reign until he has put all his enemies under his feet. The last enemy to be destroyed is death" (1 Corinthians 15:24–26 NIV). COVID-19 is death, and God has conquered death. "He will swallow up death in victory; and the LORD GOD will wipe away tears from off all faces; and the rebuke of his people shall he take away from all the earth: for the LORD hath spoken it" (Isaiah 25:8). Many churches are not open or only allowing a few people inside and streaming online.

Day Ninety-One

April 13, 2020

We are suffering through plagues, storms, and wildfires, the earth is groaning because God's people have been disobedient. We have broken our covenant with God by not giving Him our best. "'A son honors his father, and a slave his master. If I am a father, where is the honor due me? If I am a master, where is the respect due me?' says the LORD Almighty. 'It is you priests who show contempt for my name. But you ask, "How have we shown contempt or your name?" By offering defiled food on my altar. But you ask, "How have we defiled you?" By saying that the LORD'S table is contemptible. When you offer blind animals for sacrifice, is that not wrong? When you sacrifice lame or diseased animals, is that not wrong? Try offering them to your governor! Would he be pleased with you? Would he accept you?' says the LORD Almighty. 'Now plead with God to be gracious to us. With Such offerings from your hands, will he accept you?' says the LORD Almighty. 'Oh, that one of you would shut the temple doors, so that you would not light useless fires on my altar! I am not pleased with you,' says the LORD Almighty, 'and I will accept no offering from your hands.

217

My name will be great among the nations, from where the sun rises to where it sets. In every place incense and pure offerings will be brought to me, because my name will be great among the nations,' says the LORD Almighty. 'But you profane it by saying, "The LORD's table is defiled," and, "Its food is contemptible." And you say, "What a burden!" and you sniff at it contemptuously,' says the LORD Almighty. 'When you bring injured, lame or diseased animals and offer them as sacrifices, should I accept them from your hands?' says the LORD. 'Cursed is the cheat who has an acceptable male in his flock and vows to give it, but then sacrifices a blemished animal to the Lord. For I am a great king,' says the LORD Almighty, 'and my name is to be feared among the nations'" (Malachi 1:6–14 NIV).

We have broken our covenant with God, by not keeping His ways, by not honoring God. "'And now, you priests, this warning is for you. If you do not listen, and if you do not resolve to honor my name,' says the LORD Almighty, 'I will send a curse on you, and I will curse your blessings. Yes, I have already cursed them, because you have not resolved to honor me. Because of you I will rebuke your descendants; I will smear on your faces the dung from your festival sacrifices, and you will be carried off with it. And you will know that I have sent you this warning so that my covenant with Levi may continue,' says the LORD Almighty. 'My covenant was with him, a covenant of life and peace, and I gave them to him; this called for reverence and he revered me and stood in awe of my name. True instruction was in his mouth and nothing false was found on his lips. He walked with me in peace and uprightness, and turned many from sin. For the lips of the priest ought to preserve knowledge, because he is the messenger of the LORD Almighty and people seek instruction from his mouth. But you have turned from the way and by your teaching have caused many to stumble; you have violated the covenant with Levi,' says the LORD Almighty. 'So I have caused you to be despised and humiliated before all the people, because you have not followed my ways but have shown partiality in matters of the law'" (Malachi 2:1-9 NIV).

We have broken our covenant with God by being unfaithful. "Do we not all have one Father? Did not God create us? Why do we profane the covenant of our ancestors by being unfaithful to one another? Judah has been unfaithful. A detestable thing has been committed in Israel and in Jerusalem: Judah has desecrated the sanctuary the LORD loves by marrying women who worship a foreign god. As for the man who does this, whoever he may be, may the LORD remove him from the tents of Jacob—even though he brings an offering to the LORD Almighty. Another thing you do: You flood the LORD's altar with tears. You weep and wail because he no longer looks with favor on your offerings or accepts them with pleasure from your hands. You ask, 'Why?' It is because the LORD is the witness between you and the wife of your youth. You have been unfaithful to her, though she is your partner, the wife of your marriage covenant. Has not the one God made you? You belong to him in body and spirit. And what does the one God seek? Godly offspring. So be on guard, and do not be unfaithful to the wife of your youth. 'The man who hates and divorces his wife,' says the LORD, the God of Israel, 'does violence to the one he should protect,' says the LORD Almighty" (Malachi 2:10–16 NIV).

We have broken our covenant with God through injustice. "You have wearied the LORD with your words. 'How have we wearied him?' you ask. By saying, 'All who do evil are good in the eyes of the LORD, and he is pleased with them' or 'Where is the God of justice?'" (Malachi 2:17 NIV). We have broken covenant with God by withholding our tithes. "'Ever since the time of your ancestors you have turned away from my decrees and have not kept them. Return to me, and I will return to you,' says the LORD Almighty. 'But you ask, "How are we to return?" Will a mere mortal rob God? Yet you rob me. But you ask, "How are we robbing you?" In tithes and offerings. You are under a curse—your whole nation—because you are robbing me. Bring the whole tithe into the storehouse, that there may be food in my house. Test me in this,' says the LORD Almighty, 'and see if I will not throw open the flood gates of heaven and pour out so much blessing that there will not be room enough to store it. I will prevent pests from devouring your crops, and the vines in your fields will not drop their fruit before it is ripe,' says the LORD Almighty. 'Then all the nations will call you blessed, for yours will be a delightful land,' says the LORD Almighty" (Malachi 3:7–12 NIV).

We have spoken arrogantly against God. "'You have spoken arrogantly against me,' says the LORD. 'Yet you ask, "What have we said against you?" You have said, "It is futile to serve God. What do we gain by carrying out his requirements and going about like mourners before the LORD Almighty? But now we call the arrogant blessed. Certainly evildoers prosper, and even when they put God to the test, they get away with it'" (Malachi 3:13–15 NIV). Because of our disobedience and breaking covenant with God, the wrath of God is passing judgment on His people. "'So I will come to put you on trial. I will be quick to testify against sorcerers, adulterers and perjurers, against those who defraud laborers of their wages, who oppress the widows and the fatherless, and deprive the foreigners among you of justice, but do not fear me,' says the LORD Almighty" (Malachi 3:5 NIV). The day is coming. God is passing judgment and sweeping over the earth. "'Surely the day is coming; it will burn like a furnace. All the arrogant and every evildoer will be stubble, and the day that is coming will set them on fire,' says the LORD Almighty. 'Not a root or a branch will be left to them'" (Malachi 4:1 NIV). In the day of the LORD, God will have the final triumph of good over evil (Zephaniah 1). After the sweeping, God shall remember his remnant: those who were faithful who feared the Lord. "Then those who feared the LORD talked with each other, and the LORD listened and heard. A scroll of remembrance was written in his presence concerning those who feared the LORD and honored his name. 'On the day when I act,' says the LORD Almighty, 'they will be my treasured possession. I will spare them, just as a father has compassion and spares his son who serves him. And you will again see the distinction between the righteous and the wicked, between those who serve God and those who do not'" (Malachi 3:16–18 NIV). God will renew His covenant with His remnant. "'But for you who revere my name, the sun of the righteous will rise with healing in its rays. And you will go out and frolic like well-fed calves. Then you will trample on the wicked; they will be ashes under the soles of your feet on the day when I act,' says the LORD Almighty. 'Remember the law of my servant Moses, the decrees and laws I gave him at Horeb for all Israel. See, I will send the prophet Elijah to you before that great and dreadful day of the LORD comes'" (Malachi 4:2–5 NIV). God's remnant shall inherit the earth. "'I will remove from you all who mourn over the loss of your appointed festivals, which is a burden and reproach for you. At that time I will deal with all who oppressed you. I will rescue the lame; I will gather the exiles. I will give them praise and honor in every land where they have suffered shame. At that time I will bring you home. I will give you honor and praise among all the peoples of the earth when I restore your fortunes before your very eyes,' says the Lord" (Zephaniah 3:18–20 NIV).

My youngest daughter shared her dream with me this morning that caused me to pause and reflect for a moment. In her dream she said that her father had put her out, and she barely had any money, no cell phone, and a bag with a few articles of clothing. She was standing outside, and this older woman said to her, "Three more days." She started running to get away from the woman and ended up back in the same place, and the same woman came back and said, "Two more days." She took off running again and ended up at the same place. The same woman came again and said, "One more day." She ran again, returned to the same place, and the same woman came and said, "Today, go back to the place where you were hurt." She went back to the hotel, and her father was apologizing to her. She said her sister and I came downstairs and got in the car with her father. The car took off and the lady said to her, "Follow the car." She tried to follow the car but couldn't keep up.

The woman pulled up in a car next to her and said, "You missed it. Three more days." After the three days the same older woman told her, "Go and keep running and you will receive your reward." When my daughter stopped running in the dream, she made it. She looked down and saw that she had grown up. When she looked up, she saw she had her house, her car, her pets, everything she dreamed of; she had everything. The woman came back and said, "See what happens when you follow your dreams." My daughter looked at me and said, "Mommy, I understand that had I kept running, I could have gotten there sooner." She continued to say that for her those three days represented years. She said, "I could have had it three years ago, but I had to run there more years because I missed it." Listening to my young daughter was a defining moment for me. God spoke to me through my child. Had I been obedient, I could have had what God promised me three years ago.

Day Ninety-Two

April 14, 2020

My husband always says, "It seems like bad things always happen to good people." God is cleansing the earth; being at home is not a punishment. The elderly are dying in huge numbers and people, particularly people of color are dying in huge numbers as well. If you research each group, you will see the elderly who are older primarily have health issues. The African American community for years has mostly lived in low-income areas and have had limited access to quality healthcare—most suffer from diabetes, high blood pressure, and other diseases. The majority of the Black community in the United States do not own their own automobiles and have to use public transportation to get to and from work. Therefore, exposing themselves further to be infected by COVID-19. However this virus got here or how it was spread, God allowed it. The government is trying to control it, and they are unsuccessful in that quest. The president is looking to point the blame at everyone but himself and his lack of leadership skills. President Trump is withholding funding from the WHO—the World Health Organization—because he claims that they lied about the severity of the virus. God have mercy on us all. During this season everyone is being exposed; God is revealing the hearts of the people. The truth about our government and how minorities have been poorly treated and how wealth in this country is drastically disproportionately distributed is all being exposed. This paradigm shift had to occur. The tables have been turned, and everyone will be on a level playing field.

Those who have been looked down upon will now be looked to for wisdom and guidance. The homeless in various areas now have shelter because they can no longer be on the street. People who once had money and living a life of comfort and luxury are now standing in the unemployment and food lines wondering how they will pay their mortgage, their rent. However, at the same time, God's remnant are closing on houses, moving out of hotels into mansions, and getting keys to their new homes and cars. God's remnant are starting businesses and online schools and programs. God's remnant is inheriting the earth.

Day Ninety-Three

April 15, 2020

Today I received my stimulus package. Now, under normal circumstances this would not have occurred. However, God said when you leave Egypt you will not leave empty handed. "And I will make the Egyptians favorably disposed toward this people, so that when you leave you will not go empty-handed" (Exodus 3:21 NIV). I went for my walk today. While walking I began to just have a conversation with God. I didn't have my headphones, so I probably looked crazy. I didn't even notice other people around me, and by the time I did, it really did not matter. I thank God for one of many miracles that have occurred. I don't care who is in control of the government—God is in control of the world. As I walked, I continued to love on God, through worship. While walking I was able to reflect. I thought about every major moment during my lifetime that occurred and how in the midst of calamity, destruction, hurricanes, blackouts, corrupt presidents, and terrorist attacks, I have survived. Not only did I survive, but I thrived during tragic times. God has kept me, my family. There was no lack, and it always appeared like I was thriving. I was because I knew who my source was. My faith in God had not wavered. Of course I was a few years younger than I am now. I'm married with children, my priorities shifted, my thought process shifted, there was more to worry or be concerned about. Of course there were moments where fear crept in—I'm human. However, I never forgot my source. My faith in God kept me going, and it's that same faith in God that will carry me up and out of this COVID-19 making me stronger to face another challenge. Some people are saying that these are the end times, when the truth of the matter is no one knows when Jesus is coming back. Of course there will be many signs and wonders, however, no one truly knows the day or the hour when Christ is to return, but we are to keep watch. "But about that day or hour no one knows, not even the angels in heaven nor the Son, but only the Father. As it was in the days of Noah, so it will be at the coming of the Son of Man. For in the days before the flood, people were eating and drinking, marrying and giving in marriage, up to the day Noah entered the ark; and they knew nothing about what would happen until the flood came and took them away. That is how it will be at the coming of the Son of Man. Two men will be in the field; one will be taken and the other left. Two women will be grinding with a hand mill; one will be taken and the other left. Therefore keep watch, because you do not know on what day your Lord will come. But understand this: If the owner of the house had known at what time of night the thief was coming, he would have kept watch and would not have let his house be broken into. So you also must be ready, because the Son of Man will come at an hour when you do not expect him" (Matthew 24:36–44 NIV).

This is just the beginning of things to come. I do know we have a short window to get our house in order and save our money because after this shift, another shift is coming, and business as usual will not be the same. The whole world system will be completely different. Be careful and watchful of all these people donating billions of dollars and the newspaper and television advertising "A New Normal." It is all a prelude to what those in power are trying to do. However, what they try to do and will be successful in doing will be the cause and source of their demise. Watch while praying, asking God for wisdom. You cannot depend on a man or woman for anything. Seek God and His infinite wisdom, study, and know the Word of God for yourself. Be watchful of false prophets, priests, giving you a presold or prepaid word, when the only word you need is the Word of God.

Day Ninety-Four

April 16, 2020

Soon there will be one church, one sound, one congregation. God is coming back for his church. We must repent; we have strayed too far away from God. "Yet I hold this against you: You have forsaken the love you had at first. Consider how far you have fallen! Repent and do the things you did at first. If you do not repent, I will come to you and remove your lampstand from its place. But you have this in your favor: You hate the practices of the Nicolaitans, which I also hate. Whoever has ears, let them hear what the Spirit says to the churches. To the one who is victorious, I will give the right to eat from the tree of life, which is in the paradise of God" (Revelation 2:4–7 NIV).

Day Ninety-Five

April 17, 2020

Just a few more days—we must remain calm in the midst of a storm. We cannot afford to be reactionary—no need to make hasty decisions out of impulse. Moves need to be made, however, we must wait until given the green light to go and move forward. When driving in your car there are traffic lights and stop signs on the road for a reason. Everyone must wait their turn to go. The red light means stop, the yellow light means slow down or proceed with caution. The green light means go. Everyone is going to get their green light. However, when we move too early, we can find ourselves in a potentially bad situation. If my light is red and your light is green and I start moving, I'm now putting you and everyone else around me in danger because I moved before it was my turn and my time. I am now about to cause a serious accident. I am about to cause an unnecessary event because I was not patient enough to wait my turn.

Prior to this pandemic people had plans and things scheduled that they were eager to achieve and now all of those plans are on hold. Thus far the reaction of some people is confusion, anger, pain, depression, fear, frustration, and panic. People have so many unanswered questions. One question that I continue to hear is, "Why or how long must I wait?" People are now isolated and confined to their homes, feeling like they have been punished. Prior to this pandemic, September 17, 2018, was the beginning of my isolation and transformation process. God had previously shown me what I was going to lose and what I was going to gain. Today I can honestly say that I indeed lost those material things that were revealed to me in my vision. However, I am grateful to have one of the most important possessions and that is my family, my loves, because had I not slowed down, had God not slowed me down, I would have lost everything that only God could replace.

I have been separated from my source of income, friends, and family members, not to be punished. I was separated and put into isolation to be prepared for what was coming, to go through this transformation process so I could fulfill my divine purpose. God said to me people will not understand how, why, what, or when this process of transformation is complete. The question to be answered is, "How did I get to my place in God? What did I do to get where I am?" The future has already been written for us. God has written the beginning, middle, and our ending—he knows what we will face along our journey. I know what is waiting for me on the other side, now I just have to go through the storms, tornadoes, and earthquakes. I have to survive COVID-19 and spend two, almost three, years living in a hotel. I have to obey God and trust him, not knowing sometimes how I am going to feed my children, put gas in the car, or pay my bills. I am not knowing but trusting that once

I talk to my Father in heaven, he answers, and I don't have to wait long for him to respond. Every day my needs are supplied.

Day Ninety-Six

Glory to God, that is all I can say, Glory to God. I was chatting with a former coworker and friend, and we talked briefly, checking in to see how everyone was doing in the midst of this pandemic. However, while talking, they made a statement that had me saying, "Wow." They were aware of my current situation of losing my job and having my disabled husband having to find another source of income to assist our family because the income I was receiving was gone. They were aware that I was no longer receiving comp benefits, and I had just started my project. However, I had not yielded enough fruit from my labor to supplement or replace income that was lost. So now along with so many others, my former colleagues and friends are finding themselves in a similar situation as myself and my family, of figuring out what to do next.

Now that I no longer have a 9-5 job, my bills still need to be paid, food still needs to be put on the table, clothes need to be washed, I still need toiletries and hygiene care products. Life is still happening. What should I do next? I received my stimulus check when I filed taxes and had direct deposit, but the money paid a bill or two. I filed for unemployment or attempted to file and that didn't come through. What should I do next? For me the answer was easy. My next move was to seek God and His infinite wisdom, put my face in the Word of God, be still, and listen for His voice. God is definitely speaking if you just be still, listen, and obey. So, when my former colleague said to me, "I admire you for putting it all together and making it work." My response was my faith in God kept me and my family. It was my faith in God that fueled my desire to complete my project and continue to pursue my dreams. I held on to my faith, and to whoever is reading this right now, that is my message to you.

Hold on to your faith, don't give up, don't give in, keep pushing. Yes, you will be knocked down. Yes, you will be kicked, left for dead, abandoned by people you thought would be there forever. Yes, you will experience loss and pain, some things you may never fully heal from or even forget but don't let it ruin you. Don't let your rough experiences make you bitter, but say to yourself, today I will be better. Every day you wake up is a new day to start over. "I will be better" and every day you say, "I will be better," you will notice you start saying, "I am better. I survived the storm, I survived the loss, I survived the death, I survived to be better, and now I will help someone else become better." If you are reading this today, you made it. You survived, you came out better to help someone else along the way, who is struggling to find their way out of bitterness, and into better. Everyday there will be a fight, a challenge, but now you know how to survive and conquer. "For I know that with Jesus on our side, things will work out fine. We're going to make it" (Rev. Timothy Wright).

Day Ninety-Seven

April 19, 2020

The people behind the scenes may never get recognized by man. God sees all and will reward you openly. God is a rewarder of those who diligently seek him. "But without faith it is impossible to please him: for he that cometh to God must believe that he is, and that he is a rewarder of them that diligently seek him" (Hebrews 11:6).

Day Ninety-Eight

April 20, 2020

I understood upon embarking on this journey that there would be lives lost and changed because of everything happening around us. This paradigm shift had to occur. Although God allowed me to see people dying, He did not show me how they would die. I stated earlier during this pandemic many people would die from the virus, however, there will be many more passing during this time from different causes. So, I was prepared for death, however, I was not prepared for the impact or effect these mass deaths would have on me mentally, emotionally, even physically. We must continue to pray and trust God. God does not make mistakes. I feel this closer to home, in my family. I know I shouldn't put things in the atmosphere, and I'm praying for my entire family to remain protected and covered from this pandemic. The end of this pandemic is near, however, the wrath of God is not complete. There is more to come after this. We must repent and come back into alignment.

Day Ninety-Nine

April 21, 2020

God is sweeping over the earth. There is only a small remnant of people left to lead God's people. God's remnant shall inherit the earth. God's remnant is replacing those who have left the earth. People are baffled, not comprehending why certain people are leaving, nor have they expected that those who have already left to be gone. Churches are losing leaders, governments are losing officials in high places. God is replacing these people with His remnant.

Day One Hundred

April 22, 2020

Today is the hundredth day of this one-hundred-day journey. The current time now is 12:35 a.m. Something unexplainable is about to happen: a miracle. I shared with my husband that God put us in position for a miracle. Everything that has happened to us was to position us for what was coming. Losing my job two years ago was to put us in position. We had to experience what so many people are experiencing now due to COVID-19, to have us already in place. We had to lose our home and main source of income, we had to move into a hotel and apply for assistance to already be in place. Because had these things not occurred two years ago, we would be waiting for unemployment, food, health benefits, or looking for shelter like the hundreds and thousands of people who are now finding themselves in the same situation. However, the difference in our situation is that we are content where we are and we have learned how to adjust and have gotten closer together as a family, drawing closer to God.

We are learning to find peace in the midst of a storm. We have been isolated, in order to grow. God has hidden us to spiritually mature us. Isolation is necessary for growth; it was necessary to go through the transformation process. I must say that I stepped out too soon, and I had to go back in. God is about to show his mighty power. Glory to the Lamb of God! It was imperative that during this process we had to change. However, when God lifts his hand and this pandemic dries up, we cannot go back to our old lifestyles. I understand that I have a profound impact on everyone I encounter, especially my family. It is my prayer that when I go back out and see the faces of the people and their state of being, because the paradigm shift has occurred, the hearts and minds of the people would have changed.

Reflections

April 23, 2020

Yesterday was the last day of the one-hundred-day journey. Although this part of the journey is complete, it was just the beginning of the transformation process. At the beginning of this journey, I stated that even in the midst of everything happening around us, there will be miracles and there were miracles. People that I had prayed for have continued to call and text about all the miracles that they have been experiencing. I had prayed to God asking that before God blessed me, to bless them, do it for them before you do it for me. God has done it for them, and I praised God in thanksgiving for each of them. I stopped to look and realized that for every person I prayed for, I was experiencing a similar issue within my marriage, my finances, even a dwelling place for my family, so I prayed for each individual and family asking God to do it for them and said, "If God did for them, he will do it for me." Miracles continued to occur even up to the one-hundredth day, I received a message about another person receiving an unexpected blessing, and I rejoiced with them.

I was excited because I knew I was next—my family was next to be blessed. However, I understood that blessings were not going to happen if I wasn't obedient and followed instructions and did what was necessary to get to where we needed to be. I had to first learn how to be content with where God had me. I had to pull my family in closer to God, we had to recalibrate, realign ourselves within the will of God. My husband didn't understand why I kept helping people, knowing they were not doing the same for me. I told my husband it is not about people doing the same in return. I said it's about planting a seed, sowing into the life of that person and showing kindness, and that one day we will be rewarded by God. By being obedient God will bless us. I said, "One planteth, another watereth and God gives the increase."

"I planted the seed, Apollos watered it, but God has been making it grow. So neither the one who plants nor the one who waters is anything, but only God, who makes things grow. The one who plants and the one who waters have one purpose, and they will each be rewarded according to their own labor. For we are coworkers in God's service; you are God's field, God's building" (1 Corinthians 3:6-9 NIV).

A lot happened while praying in the basement. I went in there and shut the door, and I cried out to God, and He heard me. "But when you pray, go into your room, close the door and pray to your Father, who is unseen. Then your Father, who sees what is done in secret, will reward you" (Matthew 6:6 NIV). Amen. Glory to the Lamb of God. When my faith should have decreased because of my current state, it has increased. I believe the Word of God, for it is the only thing that I have to stand on. People see my situation and expect me to be sad or depressed. Or they will say things like, "Don't look for a miracle, accept that what you are in is real and figure out how to get out of it. You got yourself in it, now get yourself out of it."

April 27, 2020

It has been five days since the completion of my one-hundred-day journey. However, five days later and the journey continues, until we get with the program. I was praying aloud, telling God that I was ready for my miracle, and my youngest daughter said, "Well, that is not going to happen until you get with the program." "We all have to get with the program." She said, "I just heard get with the program." So I asked, "Well, what is the program?" She said, "You have to get through whatever you are going through. Daddy has to get through whatever he's going through. I have to get through whatever I'm going through and my sister has to get through hers too. Until we get over whatever we are going through we will stay on level one. So can ya'll just hurry up so we can get out of here." I asked her where she was, and she said, "I'm in the middle, that's why I started writing poems about y'all." That conversation with my youngest child was profound, and I pray that God assists me with raising her and her sister, nurturing both of their gifts. We have to get through it but when we come out, we are going to be better and new people. Glory to the Lamb of God: "Out of the mouth of babes flows wisdom." Clearly God has spoken to me through my child to inform me that I have not fully completed my transformation process.

May 5, 2020

It is now thirteen days after the one-hundred-day journey, and I am disappointed with myself. I allowed myself to slip backward within my mind. Everything dead is just that dead, and I can no longer afford to entertain dead things. We cannot continue to return to things that were toxic from the start and will continue to remain toxic. The journey will continue until we completely change.

May 7, 2020

Fifteen days after the one-hundred-day journey, people don't want truth. People are comfortable in the world they have created for themselves because in reality they are actually unstable. We have to be careful not to come out too soon. Because you have a few good days, weeks, or months, do not translate that you are completely delivered or have truly transformed. Resistance from completing your transformation process will delay your blessing and process of coming out better than who you were when you first went in.

January 14, 2021

Today marks three hundred and sixty-five days since the beginning of my one-hundred-day journey that started on January 14, 2020.

Since the completion of those one hundred days a lot has transpired. We are in our full year of COVID-19; the cases and deaths have skyrocketed. There were approvals of two vaccines that are slowly making its way throughout the United States. Other countries around the world have developed a rapid system to distribute the vaccine. However, the United States continues to struggle with addressing the virus or any relief for people. Truthfully I don't know if they really know if the vaccines will be effective, they rolled them out so quickly, yet slowly, because a new strand has already formed, and they will need a vaccine for that. My family and I will continue to take Communion twice, maybe three times a week, along with my vitamins, supplements, and prayer as our vaccination for now. We haven't had a flu shot in over a year, and God has been keeping us. I will admit, I drink cod liver oil in a shot glass and chase the kids around to have them take it as well.

Since the one-hundred-day journey, we have witnessed years of racism, bigotry, and prejudice being uncovered and exposed. There is a definite shift, a paradigm shift that has occurred, and God's remnant is finally going to take their rightful place. The president & vice president elect are Joe Biden and Kamala Harris. The current president doesn't want to concede and has ignited a fire on January 6, 2021 in White militia and various hate groups who were waiting for the day to unleash their lawless behavior freely without any consequences or so they thought. Justice will soon come. God has heard the prayers and cries of His people, and

He is now walking through the earth uncovering and striking down everything that is unfit for this paradigm shift. Change is inevitable.

There is war and division within governmental systems, and people are still dying by the hands of law enforcement. Hospitals are overrun with COVID-19 patients. The fate of who lives or dies is in the hands of doctors and medical facilities who don't have enough resources to save everyone. But even in the midst of all of this, God's remnant is covered and protected, thriving in the pandemic. There is truly safety in Goshen.

References

Baruch, R. (2015). Hebrew Numerology and The Bible loveisrael.org/articles/2015/11/13/hebrew-numerology-and-the-bible

King James Bible. (2020). King James Bible Online.
https://www.kingjamesbibleonline.org

Merriam-Webster (2021). Destiny. Merriam-Webster.com dictionary. Merriam-Webster.
https://www.merriam-webster.com/dictionary/destiny

New International Version. (2011). Zondervan
Grand Rapids, Michigan (1973).

The Teacher's Bible Commentary (1972). Broadman Press
Nashville, Tennessee.

Understanding Biblical Numbers (2015).
Harvestime International Network
http://www.harvestime.org